How to Live with A *Jewish* Cat #2

by
Sig and Pat Heavilin

Illustrations by Cher Selleck

❖ **CEREBRAL HOLLOW PRESS** ❖

In remembrance
Irving Martin, a true mensch
1900 – 1994

Cerebral Hollow Press Edition 1997

Copyright © 1996 by Sig and Pat Heavilin

All rights reserved. No part of this book may be reproduced by any process without the written permission of the copyright holders.

Queries regarding rights and permissions should be addressed to: Cerebral Hollow Press, 890-75 Robinhood Drive, Reno, NV 89509-4672.

In accordance with stringent dietary laws, less than 2% of the schmaltz in this book was previously published in *How to Live with a Jewish Cat* © 1994 by Cerebral Hollow Press.

Designed by Carousel Graphics
of Sparks, NV

Manufactured in the United States of America

ISBN 0-9643050-1-1

ACKNOWLEDGEMENTS

Freud, Jung, Adler (not the harmonica player) and Dr. R.A. Heavilin, a shrink in Connecticut who also does not work cheap.

To Jay Quetnick who, as an employer, gave us 10 of the best years of our lives, culminating in our marriage.

To Herb Caen of *The San Francisco Chronicle*, a newspaperman's newspaperman.

To Rhoda Herzoff of *The Chicago Jewish News* for persuading us to write this sequel.

Laura G. Leautier, D.V.M., for her invaluable research.

The entire staff of The Washoe County Library, NV, for tracking down all manner of obscure materials for us.

"Cats and monkeys, monkeys and cats—
all human life is there."

—William James (1842 – 1910)
U.S. psychologist and philosopher

Contents

Introduction

Part I: How to Communicate with Your Cat
1. How to Shmooze with Your Cat Through Interspecies Telepathy — 9
2. How to Hypnotize Your Cat — 15

Part II: How to Diagnose Your Cat's Mental Disorders
3. C.A.T.N.I.P.: Cats' Alpha Tests: Neuroses, Intelligence & Personality — 20
4. How to Interpret Your Cat's Dreams — 36

Part III: Case Histories of Dysfunctional Felines
5. The Oedipuss Complex — 43
6. Littermate Rivalry — 49
7. Cats Who Love Too Much (co-dependency) — 52
8. Case History of an Idiot Savant — 57
9. Past Life Recall, Possession — 63
10. Multiple Puss-onalities — 70
11. Feline Stress Syndrome — 77

Part IV: How to Choose and Implement Psychotherapies for Your Cat
12. Primal Meow & Primal Paw Painting Therapies — 85
13. Alternative Therapies for Your Crazy Cat — 96
14. I Love You, Allis Chalmers — 109

Dictionary of Psychiatric Terms — 116

Translations of Yiddish Terms and Phrases — 121
(They are italicized throughout the book)

INTRODUCTION

Hail the return of the Jewish cat! This ambitious sequel is devoted exclusively to the *meshugeh* cat. Is there any other kind? In fact, one of the contributors to this seminal work is Judi Lashnits, co-author of *Is Your Cat Crazy?*, published by Macmillan. As you might have guessed, the answer to Judi's question is almost always a resounding, "Funny you should ask."

Especially is *meshugehness* characteristic of the Jewish feline, the product of centuries of *tummel*. There was that business with the Egyptians and being shlepped from country to country ever since, always burdened by the emotional baggage called angst or sometimes, "The Woody Allen Syndrome."

To such cats is this book dedicated with the premise that psychiatry is uniquely suited to modifying the behavior of dysfunctional felines, be they Orthodox, Conservative or Reform. Why psychiatry? Because it is to Jewishness what Beethoven's Ninth is to a symphony orchestra.

This has been true since Biblical times. In ancient Egypt, a Pharaoh summoned Joseph and said, "No offense intended, but your coat of many colors is driving me crazy."

Joseph gestured to a divan upholstered with gold brocade, beside which stood a matching chair.

"Lie down, Mr. Pharaoh," said Joseph, "and I'll sit next to you."

This done, Joseph placed a clock on an end table and said, "Okay, kiddo, say the very first thing that comes to mind."

This anecdote does not appear in the Bible and, curiously, references to cats are also conspicuously absent from both the Old and New Testaments. In the former, dogs are mentioned frequently though derogatorily. They were regarded as loathsome scavengers.

Why were cats ignored by the scribes of old? Most likely because felines are secretive and uninformative, reluctant to reveal their inner selves.

Modestly, we submit that this book will bridge the communication gap between Man and Cat by enabling readers to access their pets' thoughts, analyze their problems and solve them by functioning as their cat's psychotherapists.

Of course today you can take your cat to an animal behaviorist. But it will cost...! Joseph charged that Pharaoh 9.95 shekels an hour and very quickly acquired a new coat of many colors—silver fox, red marten, black sable, white ermine, and starlight, pastel and nutria mink.

By playing Freud to your Freudycat, you too can save enough money to purchase a fancy-shmancy coat. And if you mail us the back cover of this book, we'll give you 50% off on cleaning, glazing and cold storage. What are friends for?

Now then, pick up your cat, place it on a couch and give him/her the "kiddo" routine. It *will* work. Trust us.

Sig & Pat

Chapter 1

How to *Shmooze* with Your Cat Through Interspecies Telepathy

Inarguably, this is the most important chapter in this book. Unless you learn to communicate with your cat through the process of telepathy, you will be unable to diagnose its problems, prescribe treatment and function as its therapist. *

Although you may view the concept of interspecies telepathic communication with considerable dubiety, cats and all other animals have shared their thoughts and feelings with homo sapiens ever since we ape-like animals shinnied down a tree and formulated language.

---

* There is no reason to proceed with this chapter if daily dialogues are already a part of your relationship with your pet, especially if your level of communication has attained a sophisticated level, e.g., discussions of such lofty sociopolitical works as Plato's *Republic,* Thoreau's *Walden,* Harold Laski's *Liberty in the Modern State.*

History supports this contention. In an ancient Aztec temple there is a painting of Quetzalcoatl, the feathered serpent god, telepathically asking a moneyed Guatemalan cat to lend him a couple of quetzals until Friday.

Getting on line with your cat requires patience, patience and more patience. Initially, your goal is to transmit visual images to your cat, not words or thoughts. It is best to practice on lower life forms. Because almost nobody bothers with them, they will be eager to respond. Here's a step by step guide to communicating with ants:

Lay face down on an ants' nest. Will yourself to believe that you are one of the colony's employees. Project the image of yourself in chitinous clothing and hard hat, lunch pail in hand, asking the shift supervisor for a work assignment. Do not— repeat, *do not*—try to project a series of words: *"Hi, boss. Sorry I'm late. Well, what's on the schedule today?"* Remember, images, unlike specific languages, are universal.

Repeat this exercise daily. Don't expect a response for a month or so. Your very presence will alarm and confuse the ants. Eventually, they will "get the picture." Yes, when you have all but given up hope of receiving a "video" from the insects, they will project an image to you. It may depict you removing the carcass of a dung beetle that has for some weeks blocked access to Delta tunnel. Or leading them to a picnic site.

In terms of invertebrates, our most difficult "breakthrough" involved an anaconda. Frustrated by the reptile's refusal to reveal its thoughts, we attached to its scales a hypersensitive microcomponent electroencephalography device, galvanic skin sensors, a Doppler ultrasound transducer and a Sharper Image micro-recorder. The snake twitched and projected images to us which said, in effect, "Get this crap off me. You want to talk? We'll talk."

Shmoozing with Your Cat

Easier by far is it to communicate with, say, an earthworm, who regards you as a novelty, than a cat who takes you for granted. Indeed, some cats are really into being haughty, self-centered felines and will not so much as flash you the time of day. But, if you are fortunate, your cat may have been a human in a previous life and will relish an opportunity to shmooze with you.

Begin by forming a simple thought, pictorialize it in your mind and imagine it traveling through space—pixel by pixel, if you are a technonerd—and being received by your animal friend. Allow your imagination to insist that the message reached its destination. Then imagine receiving an answer. After repeated attempts you *will* receive an answer expressed as an idea, concept or expression of feeling.

Below are simple statements and questions to direct to your cat and the images that will encourage the cat to respond.

YOUR THOUGHT	THE PICTURE YOU PROJECT
"Are you hungry?"	Cat gnawing on a grouper.
"Are you hot?"	Nubian slave fans cat with palm fronds.
"Shall we play?"	A mah-jonng set.
"Did you use your litterbox?"	Cat buried up to its neck in sand.

"Do you wish to be groomed?"	A hair stylist, comb in hand.
"Did you have a nice day?"	A series of smiley faces with question marks.
"Are you cold?"	Cat shoveling its way out of a snowdrift.
"While I'm vacationing, Joyce will look in on you."	Joyce bearing toys and *noshes*.
"Are you thirsty?"	Cat drinking from Norway's Mardalsfossen waterfalls.
"Shall we curl up in bed together and watch TV?"	Cat hogging the bed, obstructing your view of the television set.

In time, your cat will reply by projecting images of its own. They may be direct answers to your questions, e.g., representations of choice morsels, an electric blanket or back-scratcher. Cat's comments, however, will not necessarily be cutesy-pie. Sometimes when we bombard our cat with thoughts, he responds with a picture of us being burned at the stake.

From simple images you can progress to highly detailed ones. The battle of Thermopylae (480 B.C.) was decided by an Abyssinian cat who provided Xerxes, leader of the Achaemenid army, with telepathic "pictures" of the deployment of troops by Spartan chieftain Leonidas. A double agent, the cat also sold reconnaissance photos—concealed in knishes—to the Greeks. When his duplicity was exposed, the feline fled to an Orthodox rabbinate and became known as Rov Rabyssinian.

As your mastery of interspecies telepathy improves, you may one day find that you can transmit verbalized thoughts to your pet by using a language of its choice, for each breed of cat and each species of animal, has its own vocabulary. The most satisfactory means of learning your cat's preferred language is to study with an animal-linguist.

Some common feline lexicons include Burmese, Siamese, Persian, Himalayan, Tonkinese, Russian, Balinese, Singapura and the pungent tongue of the alley cat, Gutter Talk.

A universal cat language has also asserted itself as more and more felines have, in recent years, been expatriated. Akin to Esperanto, the international vocabulary is called "Katsch" and has a Yiddish lilt. In Katsch, the word for cocklebur is "Aarrgh!"

Many other animal species have their own language.*

In summary, you *can* communicate with your cat. It takes time and infinite patience but one day, with a telegraphic mouse click, a window will open and you find yourself logged on in "tiger space." This done, you will be able to talk and walk your dysfunctional cat down the path of recovery.

It is *bashert*.

* Some examples: Llaman ; Emu-ish (Reform and Orthodox); Old Yak, New Yak; Hensh (also spoken by roosters); Platypusarian; Sow and Pig Latin; Assic (includes mules); Giraffiti; Antenna-nyms & Hum-onyms (bees); Thesaurus (most prehistoric animals); Baa Baa Rhum (tipsy sheep).

References

Goodall, J. (1990). Communicating with Owls Who Don't Give a Hoot. *Avian Books*.

Edge, Getthe (1992). One Hundred One-Letter Words You Can Use Playing Mind Games—or Scrabble. *Mensa Society*. April-May.

Krishna, Hairy (1988). Telepathy as a Tool for Determining If Your Cat Is a Smurf. *Tibetan Scrolls*.

Chapter 2

How to Hypnotize Your Cat

This chapter presumes that you have learned to *shmooze* with your cat telepathically. If you haven't, hypnotizing your cat may help you reach that goal. Once lulled into a trance, cats can be instructed to visually project their thoughts to you; telepathy and hypnosis are interwoven as examples of mind control. Before attempting to hypnotize your pet, here are some general do's and don'ts:

Do—

Choose ambient surroundings for your hypnotherapy sessions. Your cat will be less responsive in a Motel 6 near the Lincoln Tunnel than in a suite at the Tel Aviv Hilton (at 3,000 New Sheqalim per day).

Offer your cat a reward for its cooperation—an Alfa Romeo, chicken gizzards or *The Collected Letters of Isaac Bashevis Singer,* depending on its body/personality type.*

Strive to maintain a balance between being everyday friendly and crisply professional. If your cat has a belittling name, like *"Klutz"* refer to it as "Hey, you."

Have handy a list of questions you wish to ask your cat when it is "under." "Do you *really* like me?" And then, "So how much?"

If your self-esteem proves lower than your cat's, you may decide to reverse roles.

Prepare a list of suggestions for modifying your cat's behavior and be specific. "You will no longer find yourself compelled to wear a Mighty Morphin Power Ranger costume and kick butt."

---

* Based on Ernst Kretschmer's "Theory of Constitutionality," cats' physiques and corresponding temperaments fell into these major categories: Ectomorphic: light boned and adept at epee fencing; Endomorphic: intellectual cats of medium build who prefer *The N.Y. Times Literary Review* to *The Reader's Digest*; Pyknic: round-bodied bullies who enjoy sumo wrestling with ectomorphs.

Don't attempt to hypnotize your cat—

If your pet is asleep, falling asleep or emerging from sleep. These conditions may rule out hypnosis altogether.

If your cat is counting money, engaged in bathroom behavior or sexual activity. (This rule also applies to humans.)

If your cat wears tinted contact lenses.

If your cat is zonked on Elavil, Zoloft or mushrooms purchased from anyone named Running Deer.

If your cat is under the influence of *The 1812 Overture*.

Putting your cat in a trance is called induction. The basic methods are visual fixation and verbal persuasion. As noted earlier, neither will succeed unless your cat is alert and focused.

The visual fixation method is passé. Still, it works and consists of transfixing the cat by swinging an object before its eyes in a pendulum-like motion. Hypnotists of old favored gold watch fobs. You can substitute a Lender's bagel, paperweight with built-in snowflakes, CD Rom, horseshoe crab—well, the possibilities are endless.

Swing the object six inches in front of the cat's head and at cat's eye level. At first, your cat may lash out at the pendulum but it will soon weary of the game and succumb to your will.

The patter accompanying this exercise is all important. Your voice must "swing" in time with the pendulum. Out of boredom—or eye strain—the cat's resistance will ebb and hypnosis will have been achieved.

>YOU: Pretty kitty, watch the thing, on a string, to and fro, see it go, peek and peep, fall asleep, pretty kitty, etc.

Some cats will sway from side to side like a pendulum for several hours after being hypnotized by the visual fixation method. Chancing upon such a cat, a rabbi asked, "Are you *davening* sideways?"
"No, I'm keeping time," replied the cat.
"So tell me the time."
"It's four–twenty."
"Not so," said the rabbi, consulting his watch. "It's five o'clock."
"*Oy, vay,*" said the cat, accelerating his motion. "Faster I'll have to go!"
Most therapists employ verbal persuasion. It consists of luring the cat into a dreamlike state through suggestion. There are many approaches, all similar.

>YOU: Take a deep breath, little kitty.
>CAT: Wheesh.
>YOU: Exhale.
>CAT: Whoosh.
>YOU: Breathe more deeply.
>CAT: Wheeeesh.
>YOU: Exhale.
>CAT: Whoooosh.
>YOU: You are floating, pretty kitty. Drifting. Gliding

on a gentle current in a tranquil stream. A ripple appears on the water. It spreads. A second ripple appears. Then another. A crocodile surfaces. You are one of its favorite food groups. But if you sleep and drift he will not notice you. The ripples are relaxing you. They spread from your eyes across the muscles of your forehead and your jaws. Around your back, your neck, your paws, your legs, your tummy. So soothing. You are drowsy. Very drowsy. You are asleep and safe from the crocodile. Now you will obey my every command."

If hypnosis does not work in the privacy of your home, visit Africa and float your cat on the Congo where real crocodiles thrive.

Post-hypnotic Suggestion

By prearrangement, you can command your cat to lapse into a trance anytime, anywhere. All that is required is a signal that you have conveyed to your cat during a previous hypnosis. Perhaps you told your cat, when it was last entranced, that it would fall asleep whenever it hears you say "Russian Tea Room" or "Menasha Skulnik." It's a real power trip for you—and what cat doesn't welcome an excuse to close its eyes?

References

Murdock, Iris (1991). If Looks Could Kill, My Hypnotist Would be Dead. *Bedtime/Warner.*

Wynken, Blynken & Nod (1994). How to Stare Down a Cat. *Focus Books.*

Svengali, Z.Z. (1990). Everything I Know About Hypnosis I Learned from My Pupils. *Vitreous Humor. Vol. II.*

Chapter 3

**C.A.T.N.I.P.: Cats' Alpha Tests:
Neuroses, Intelligence & Personality**

Finally, a single battery of test that will enable you to learn everything you need to know about your cat! Is it smart? Dumb? Introverted? Extroverted? Well-adjusted? Neurotic?

The product of years of arduous experimentation and research, C.A.T.N.I.P. was developed by the team of psychometrists that designed Rorschach bubble gum cards for juvenile delinquents, encephalographs disguised as Walkman radios and "Blab," a line of soft drinks laced with truth serum.

The subjects included 209 cats from all walks of life—e.g., Maine Cohen cats, cats in Federal penitentiaries, cats hooked on phonics and a random sample (a cat named "Random," owned by Emilie Sample, a root beer bottler).

The cats were divided into three experimental groups: newly born, nearly dead and "Yo!" Owners skilled in telepathic communication answered the true-or-false questions below for their cats. And we ask you to do the same.

TEST I

Does your cat—

1. Think *Jesus Christ Superstar* is a better show than *Fiddler on the Roof*?
2. Want to hunt members of the Audubon Society?
3. Think you should consult a speech therapist because you can't purr?
4. Fidget at the sound of advancing artillery fire?
5. Resent sharing its bath with a rubber duck?
6. Aspire to write a cookbook titled, *"The Best of Bambi"*?
7. Favor toxic waste dumping at dog pounds?
8. Regard face-to-face intercourse as psychopathic behavior?
9. Stir fry small animals?
10. Conceptualize death as being a nice, long nap without a wake-up call?
11. Think it's kosher to eat ribs at Mel's Donner Pass Diner?
12. Refuse to augment its income by teaching?

13. Find itself depressed by bouts of euphoria?
14. Balk at submitting to electroshock therapy if the technician is wearing a hood?
15. Eat out of a giant satellite dish?
16. Think it immoral to nap during the daytime?
17. Prefer the sound of a shofar to that of a can opener?
18. Consider *Goy*-a a better painter than Marc Chagall?
19. Prefer Veg-a-matic Infomercials to National Geographic wild life specials?
20. Refuse to curtsy to Queen Elizabeth?
21. Chew your fingernails and swallow them?
22. Brush after every meal or, at least, comb?
23. Wear bumper stickers on his/her heinie?
24. Think Ann Page mayonnaise is superior to Helmann's?

25. Believe Bastet, sacred cat of Egypt, was an illegitimate child?
26. Want to dig up the bones buried by the Rottweiler who lives next door?
27. Pee against fire hydrants?
28. Think anyone is as *goyisha* as Nancy Reagan—or Marie Osmond?
29. Craves personal knowledge of how many billion hamburgers McDonald's has *really* served?
30. Insist White House cat Socks secretly wears pantyhose?
31. Believe that all things are real, including Elvis impersonators?

32. Want a bidet installed in her litter box?
33. Interpret all of Rorschach's ink blots as stupid ink blots?
34. Rate *Over the Waves* as a catchier tune than *Who Stole the Kishka?*
35. Rationalize that what it does is less important than who gets blamed?
36. Correspond with cats on S.P.C.A.'s death row?

SCORING

For each *true* answer, score plus four points. Deduct four points for each *false*. If the minuses and pluses balance out as zero, you have a disgustingly well-adjusted cat. All other scores suggest your tabby may need intensive and expensive psychotherapy. Perhaps you should consider replacing your cat with a goldfish—or Pet Rock.

TEST II

Psychodiagnostic Test for Implications Of Severe Personality Disorders

For each of the illustrations that follow, we have suggested interpretations ranging from optimistic to pessimistic. Have your cat choose the scenario that it deems most reasonable.

A. The approaching train will make *schmaltz* of the cat.

B. The train's engineer, Casey Jones Hershkowitz, will recognize the cat as his long lost pet and stop just in time.

C. The train is a mirage peculiar to this area of the Gaza Strip.

A. The animal is a courage-deprived feline—okay, scaredy cat.

B. The cat is being punished for imitating the *goyim* by repairing a carburetor and driving a pick-up truck with fuzzy dice hanging from the rear view mirror.

C. The cat will be picked up by the train in illustration at left.

A. The cat is about to kick the cigarette habit—for good.

B. The cat is happy. In his next life, he'll eat, make love, eat, make love, eat, make love, etc. In Heaven? No, as a bull in Montana.

C. The prison wall should be replastered and repainted.

A. The circus is in Bayonne, N.J. The cat will be recovered somewhere off the coast of Papua.

B. In the audience, the cat's mother asks herself, "From this he makes a living?"

C. The cat regrets that it had a bowl of Sunsweet prune juice for breakfast.

A. The cat is doing a commercial for William F. Buckley, Jr.'s BBQ Sauce. Sales will benefit Hadassah.

B. A New Age medicine man is treating the cat's arthritis with an "herbal boil."

C. The cat is kosher and worries that a dairy product will be added to the same pot.

A. The *schlimazel* is about to "donate" blood.

B. The visitor is on his way to the *vash-tsimmer*.

C. A federal mattress inspector is about to arrest the cat for having removed inspection labels from the bedding.

1. Which one of the words below does not belong in this group?

   Shpritz   2¢ plain
   Egg cream   Seltzer

2. What words describe a cat who crosses a stream twice without washing?

3. If you have a male and a female cat, which *one* is of the opposite sex?

4. Match up the Jewish cats below with their favorite mode of traveling.

   Reform   a. Kohneshtoyga wagon
   Orthodox   b. Staten Island ferry
   Conservative   c. Jet plane
   Faygala   d. Pullman

5. If no one was in the Sahara to hear it, would your cat's droppings falling on a sand dune make a sound?

6. Which word does not belong in this group?

   Halvah   Hasenpfeffer
   Okra   Jerky

7. In your cat's opinion, which of the following statements most completely represents "sharing" a chicken?

   A. Owner gives cat a winglet?
   B. Owner gives thigh to cat?

  C. Owner divides fowl with cat?
  D. Owner gives entire bird to cat and sends out for Chinese?

8. Ask your cat to provide a rhyming word for each of the following. Time your cat.

  orange rhythm *gumicknuppel* June

9. Why?

10. So...?

Answers

1. So when was the last time a plain cost 2¢?

2. A dirty, double-crosser.

3. Only a rabbi could answer such a philosophical question.

4. Reform - c; Orthodox - a; Conservative - d; faygala - b

5. Yes. It would be heard by the cat doing the do-do.

6. Okra is not a food. It is pure slime made from recycled Michelin tires.

7. D.

8. June? Easy. As *gumicknuppel* in German means truncheon, luncheon would be acceptable. As for the other two, *oy!*

9. Because.

10. See answer above.

Mathematical Reasoning

1. Two cats, a British Shorthair and a Brooklyn Flatbush, board separate subway trains traveling on parallel tracks in opposite directions, train "A" at 50 mph and train "B" at 70 mph. Which of the following statements is necessarily true?

    A. The trains will pass each other and the cats will whoop gleefully.

    B. The trains will not pass each other. Pending investigation, authorities will withhold comment.

    C. A *goyisha* marine on leave will become violently ill as the result of mixing Bosco and Southern Comfort.

    D. Who cares?

2. In the course of a single holiday at Brighton, a kitten from Kent loses a draydel, three jump ropes, a beach ball, an apple knish and a ukulele. Why?

3. Kabloona, an entrepreneurial Innuit, rents igloos by the night and charges $1.00 for basic shelter, $1.50 for igloo with central heating, $2.00 for one with all amenities including a *mezuzah*, convenience bar, bed with vibrator

and X-rated videos of narwhals making "the beast with two backs." Which rental offers the most value?

4. The combined age of five of calicoat cats, as they are called in the garment district, is 16 years. Izzy is twice the age of Rose who, in turn, is the sum of the ages of Aaron and Bea. Shirley, age three, lost her whiskers while playing with a Lady Remington Razorette. Which of the following statements is valid?

- A. The cats' names are dumb.
- B. Some cats are older than others.
- C. Some cats are younger than others.
- D. Shirley's parents, represented by Robert Shapiro, are taking Lady Remington to court.

5. Does it take a cat ten times as long to catch a millipede as a centipede?

- A. Yes
- B. No
- C. Sometimes
- D. Unanswerable. Variables may apply—e.g., motivation, track conditions, steroids, footwear.

6. A cat finds three black jade beads from the K'ai-yuan period of the T'ang Dynasty on Telegraph Hill in an unimproved lot owned by Ziona Goodman, locally famous for her passamenterie, and pimento meat loaf. The cat does a *mitzvah* by delivering the beads to the adjacent Goodman residence. Ziona answers the door, introduces herself as Norma Desmond, invites the cat into her parlor and plays her favorite CD's by Papa Clutch and the Shifters, adlibbing

lyrics that accuse her husband Shlomo of having an affair with a transvestite dental hygienist. Later, the hostess shares "loco weed" and a six pack of Coors with the tabby and sings Ernie Tubbs', "There's a Tear in My Beer, Little Darlin'." The cat falls asleep. Based on the information above, which of the statements below seems most valid?

    A.   Ziona failed to serve the cat a *nosh*.
    B.   The beads were from the Han Dynasty, not the T'ang. They were *too*.
    C.   Ziona really *is* Norma Desmond.
    D.   The cat has had a trying day.

Answers

1. D.

2. Earlier on, the cat had lost all of its marbles.

3. It depends on your cat's budget and/or interest in the lustful antics of tusked sea animals.

4. D.

5. A or B as the cat may catch the millipede all at once or in increments of ten segments each, the latter method being preferred by Miss Manners.

6. B, C and D are suitable answers. A is incorrect. Fred is not a fink. A *schmuck*? Maybe.

Summary:

US: So how did your cat score on the tests?
YOU, THE READER: Don't ask!
US (SMUGLY): Just as we thought. Your cat is *meshugeh ahf toi't.*
YOU, THE READER (GLUMLY): Yes, crazy as a loon.
US (SYMPATHETICALLY): Not to worry. In the following chapters we have psychotherapies you won't believe.
YOU, THE READER: For me or my cat?
US: It's your call!

Chapter 4

How to Interpret Your Cat's Dreams

by Ludwig Luftmensch
Technical College of the Low Country, Beaufort, S.C.

Who among us has not seen a cat twitch in its sleep, paws atremble, tail switching? Observing the spectacle, we are never at loss for an explanation. "*Katzale* is dreaming that she is chasing a chipmunk or being chased by a dog." That explanation is dumb. The elements, images and icons of the furry purrer's dreams are the same as those that beguile and bedevil us when we sleep, with the curious exceptions I have listed at right.

What Cats Do Not Dream About

The War between the States	Rubick's cube
Tungsten	Pamplona, Spain
Grapefruit sections	Robert's Rules of Parliamentary Order
The Stanley Cup	Bulwer Lytton
Steatopygia	Lytton Strachey

What People Do Not Dream About

Pawing hula skirts	Being flea-dipped
Drinking from the toilet	Burying their scat
Stealth bombers and blue jays	Slinkies
Rotating lawn sprinklers	Being rescued from trees
Dumpsters behind Popeye's Chicken outlets	Being stepped on by size 11½ shoes

    The symbols in a cat's dream are the jigsaw puzzle pieces which, when properly assembled, provide a coherent interpretation of the animal's emotional problems, but one subject to the bias of the analyst. It's like recipes for brining pickles. To each his own.

A Dream
Related by Frieda, a female tortoiseshell

I dreamt I was an orphan who lived in a car wash where I buffed cars, assisted by Shamus, a sure-footed chamois. While sleepwalking within the context of my dream, Shamus and I fell in love and entered upon a life of vagabondage. Once, we served *nova* and scrambled eggs to a circle of druids. They observed that parts of the eggs were excellent.

Interpretation

This age-old dream was first related by Pepsi, a house cat, to Italian composer Vincenzo Bellini. With a quill in one hand and Pepsi in the other, "Vince" composed all three acts of the opera *La Somambula* (The Sleepwalker) between noon and the Six O'clock News one overcast day in 1831. The dream reveals an Electra conflict. Primal Meow Therapy and colonic irrigation are indicated.

A Dream
Related by Hans, a male "Heinz"

Mt. Everest towers above, its snow-mantled peak shrouded in malevolent clouds. As we prepare for our ascent, Sir Hillary and Tenzing Norkay, his Sherpa guide, make catty remarks about me behind my back. They envy my retractable claws which serve as pitons and ice axes. And they are jealous because I was outfitted by L.L. Bean and Frederick's of Hollywood. One of my porters is carrying lawn furniture and a croquet set.

The climb begins but not without acrimony. Hillary elects to take the non-smoking trail to K-2, our first encampment. Tenzing, a chain smoker, is furious. He throws his Dunhill lighter at an ibex.

The climb is hard work. My paws are numb, my whiskers sheathed in ice. I notice that my dew-claws are missing. And a bottle of gherkins.

We reach Everest's summit. Bella Abzug greets us and takes pictures of us wearing picture hats. In return, I present her with my personal convenience tray. It is very heavy because I don't believe in littering.

Interpretation

The dream reveals distorted ego boundaries as the result of premature toilet training. Alpenhorn therapy could help. It couldn't hurt.

A Dream
Related by Abe, a male shorthair

A teenage octopus from the Dry Tortugas, visiting this country as a migrant worker, comes over to my house to play. We compete at pick-up-sticks, arm wrestling, cat's cradle and juggling. The cephalopod's dexterous manipulation of its many body parts enables it to win every game.

While playing hide-and-seek, however, the octopus squeezes himself into a Panasonic Auto-Stop Pencil Sharpener, never to reappear.

The rest of the dream seems fragmented. At Wal☆Mart, I buy a homburg on sale. I am treed in Central Park by a Pembroke Welsh Corgi. I fall asleep on the subway and awake holding an authentic Stradivarius autographed by Phil Rizzuto.

Interpretation

This dream is all too familiar to animal behaviorists. In one of its many variations, the cat awakens in possession of a double indemnity insurance policy signed by Fred

MacMurray and Barbara Stanwyck. The dream reveals "tentacles envy," internalized sadistic impulses and repressed introspectionistic wishes with regard to inanimate objects. Abe is a suitable candidate for acupuncture.

A Dream
Related by Mendel, a male domestic shorthair

I am a reincarnated Dalai Lama, Trulku-la by name. The monastery over which I preside is the M.S. MANTRA RAY, a Carnival Cruise Lines ship, a seagoing Kmart enterprise.

I am hosting a banquet for guests who enter the ballroom astride yaks, singing "Hello, Dalai." A woman enters. She suffers from gout and is clad in salad greens. Identifying herself as Madam Blavatsky, the theosophist, she denounces me as being a common alley cat, a "southy" from Boston's most disreputable environs.

Even as she speaks, I find myself trying to spear an oyster with a butter knife, blowing my nose in a lobster bib and scratching my privates. At the height of my embarrassment, the ship overturns.

I am drowning. An ark draws near. Many pairs of animals crowd the rail. They laugh to see such sport as a cat dogpaddling, take Polaroid pictures and continue on their way.

My heart sinks. An enormous pelican wearing a yarmulke eyes me hungrily. The dream ends.

Interpretation

The dream reveals a sublimated fear of flying. Introverted cats are prone to this particular anxiety dream. Mendel may respond well to Medicine Lodge Drumming Therapy which is of an assertive nature.

A Dream
Related by Shelley, a Male Birman

I dream I have pulled off a series of daring drive-in crematory robberies, armed with a fire extinguisher.

The FBI (Feline Bureau of Investigation) has posted photographs of me everywhere, including cyberspace, and set bloodhounds on my trail. I am "hot," as we most wanted fugitives from justice say, and fearful that a canary who hates my guts will "sing" in exchange for a chicken feed reward.

In desperation, I undergo plastic surgery at the hands of Frankie "In-Your-Face" Physio who, as a Sephardic rabbi selling forged Dead Sea scrolls, was forced to alter his own appearance, relying on a Dremel tool, Rogaine and Retin-A. (Today he looks like Regis Philbin impersonating Howard Stern. Or vice versa.)

At this point in my dream, I am sitting up in my hospital bed with my eyes closed while Physio removes layer upon layer of bandages from my head and extracts metal staples which he drops in a nurse-held bedpan.

"Can I watch?" I ask.

"No, stupid," says Physio.

The surgeon has added insult to injury. I find myself blubbering, "You promised me cute little ears like a Scottish Fold and almond-shaped eyes like a Siamese."

Ping. Another staple falls in the pan.

"And a sort of pointy face—you know, like a Turkish Van—or Anna White, remember?" I continue.

Ping. Ping.

"Not to mention a tail tuck, liposuction of my 'as' flab. And handlebar whiskers."

More pinging before Physio sighs. "Okay, Shelley, open your eyes."

I do. The nurse hands me a mirror. I stare at the image

before me. J. Edgar Hoover stares back. He is wearing the pink negligee in which he danced at a Black Panthers' convention.

Here the dream ends. And I hide in a vacuum cleaner bag for several days.

Interpretation

The dream reveals xenophobia, a fear of foreigners, narcissistic mortification, and a persecutory identity crisis. The cat should go to the mountains and take the sun.

References

Mail, e-. (1996). Dream Recall and REM During Sleep in Microsoft Employees and Normals. *zzzz@zonked.com.*

Aculata, E.J. (1988). Wet Dreams and the Cat's Pajamas. *Orgasm Monthly. 14.* 112–134.

Lanes, The (1990). Passalong Dreams for Relay Teams. (Boxed set includes baton.) *Anchor Books.*

Figg, Newton (1992). Psychodynamics of Cats' Culinary Dreams: The Good (sprats), The Bad (over-breaded Weinerschnitzel and The Ugly (tripe a la anything). Diagnostic Food for Thought. *Journal of Feline Psycho-Gastronomy.* II

Freud, S. (1900). Dreams Are Boss—and the Grungier the Bossier. *Viennese Journal of Psychoanalysis. Vol. VII.*

Chapter 5

The Oedipuss Complex

by Dr. Robert A. Heavilin, Clinical Psychologist and Shameless Pun-ologist

Our story begins with the birth of Max the Manx. He was one of a litter born despite vigorous government efforts to keep the cat population under control ("Please do not litter"). The mother cat, Nadine, was known as "Tab" because of her predilection to collect beer can tops and slurp a certain soft drink all day. She had difficulty, however, keeping tab of her kittens, and so tried to give Max away to Frank, one of her lovers.

"No thanks. This Manx is Hank's, not Frank's!" replied Frank. Since a war injury, *bombenneurose,* dislocated his ego, Frank often used the third person, even if it did make him sound a bit like Dr. Seuss.

Back to Max. He and Hank were both stuck with the Tab, and she with them. There actually was a close physical resemblance between Max and his Dad. Others in the neighborhood would comment that Max looked like a hair o' Hank.

You can already see the direction of this case study. Worse it gets. Under normal circumstances, kittens discover their gender identity by the age of about three months. Early kittenhood. Max was no different. Unfortunately for consumers of cable television, this process occurs underground, in the unconscious mind. Here, we are grateful to the work of Dr. Sigmund Sigmoid for his work on the Oedipuss theory. Prior to his mirthful work on gender identity in felines, Sigmoid was an obsessive-compulsive proofreader who developed the sigmoidoscope to further explore colons and semicolons.

According to Sig, the male kitten unconsciously desires to mate with his mother. He really wants to get into her cat's pajamas. Freudulently, he refers to them as "pajamamas." But Max's father, Hank, does not feel threatened. Like all cool cats, he realizes that he has no competition from Max. Nevertheless—you should never take the less!—he sends a signal from his unconscious to Max's unconscious (via the UnderNet) that he (Hank) will castrate his son if he so much as purrs too long in Tab's ear. I cannot help but wonder if castration is an act of downsizing – reducing one's staff.

Remember, all this occurs at the level of the subconscious, one floor below Feline's Bargain Basement. Consciously, Max is an innocuous *nebbish*. It is beneath this placid exterior that gender development, disguised as an X-rated flick rife with incestuous intrigue, takes place.

What is Max to do? He identifies with Hank on the theory that "if you can't beat him, join him," thus continuing his development as a young male cat, accompanied by the macho chant of "Cat Man Do."*

Later on, when Max becomes an adult at the age of two years, he will fur-nicate with a female cat ("sex kitten" is the prefurred physiological term). Occasionally, because something has gone awry (in which case the actual ejaculation is refurred to as "coming through awry", a cat may copulate instead of fur-nicate, but this requires the acquiescence of the cop or sheriff's deputy involved.

Let us assume, however, that Max's sexual development proceeds according to norm (Norm, one of Dr. Sigmoid's research assistants, insisted on being in the middle of everything, so Dr. S. took the extreme measure of downsizing him to a lower case). In this case, Max begins to feel his oats during puberty. Oats is the calico cat next door and of similar age.

Unfortunately for Max, Oats is a male. This sends Max into a homophobic tailspin, and he undertakes therapy with–yes–none other than Dr. Sigmund Sigmoid! During their first session, the good doctor diagnoses Max as suffering from a dissociative identity disorder. Unable to successfully resolve his gender identity issues. Sexually confused Max switches to a different brand of cat food: Sheba for *Shabbes*. And, holy Moses, is cured!

The Electra Complex

Let us examine–"Quick, Henry, the sigmoidoscope"– the counterpart for Maxine, one of Max's sisters. During

---

* It is not clear, however, what these Asian cats *can* do. We do know that they do doo-doo and constantly struggle with their waste lines.

her early kittenhood, she wants to marry Daddy Cat. Maxine is hankering for Hank. She does not fear castration like her neurotic brother because she already is missing the thing that is castratable. Her unconscious acknowledgement that she had already been "deboned" causes no sense of dread such as Max suffers. But female felines often gather nightly, happily caterwauling, "My bone, it lives over the ocean, my bone, it lies over the sea". What Maxine and all other female kittens during this Electra stage desire unconsciously is to beget a baby by Big Daddy Cat, even though they still have their Moms to keep tabs on them. When Maxine passes through puberty into adulthood, she will "get her man" by giving birth to a "daddy" or two in her litter.

Again, this process is unconscious or below ground (grounds for analysis). At the level of consciousness, these purring female felines, during their adolescence, feel charged with libido, an old Latin word for feeling hot lust liking eating jalapeño *hamentaschen*. And indeed, when she reaches puberty, Maxine will want to fill her void with somebody's hot pepper!

This process is referred to as the Electric Complex, named after General Horace Electric, who pioneered in turning on the illumination in cat houses (why do we never worry about dog houses?). Horace used small ruby-colored bulbs. This had the side-effect of encouraging the females in these houses to be reddy for action. Also, the cat houses were easier to find, as male patrons were directed to look for the red light district.

This may have turned on Horace, but it turned off Hydra, his wife. Moreover, as he got further into the pattern of getting lit up (to keep apace with the scarlet houses, he rationalized) Hydra lit out for greener pastures, and settled in with a young apprentice named Horace Verdi (she had a thing about the name "Horace" because her father used to bet on the horaces every Saturday). There we can see the effects of an unresolved Electric complex.

What happens if your cat flunks Oedipuss I? How would you know if, indeed, this were the case? The condition, an unresolved Oedipuss crisis, would be referred to as an "Oediputz Crisis" (as in "That cat's a *putz!*") Unfortu-nately, Dr. S. provides no discussion of this pussibility, thus leaving us with a Sigmoid void. Actually Sigmund, during his teen years, tried to fill his sister's void. Her name was Rosalie and Sig luridly lured her into a large trunk. He was caught in the act and sent to reform school, thus suffering arrested adolescence. This explains why some of Sigmund's theories seem to be trunkate.

Despite Dr. Sigmoid's silence, there are some significant behavioral symptoms. If your adolescent male cat purrs obsessively in front of photographs of Grandma Moses or Lily Tomlin, this would be a sure sign of an unresolved Oedipal crisis. Other manifestations of unresolved Oediputz issues would include the compulsive reading of ancient Greek tragedies. There is some speculation that there actually was an Oedipuss Rex in ancient Greece, but further research has determined that Rex was a canine trying to pass as a feline. Now there's an identity issue!

Successful resolution of the Oedipuss crisis leads to the development of the superego. This is the internalized conscience that helps us navigate between right and wrong or right and left. In incomplete Oedipal resolution, by contrast, your cat may act unconscionably–e.g., fire bomb your home, a militant Israeli tactic. This phenomenon has come to be known, in psychoanalytic circles, as a cultural TabBoo.

What successful therapy attempts to do in these cases is to complete the Oedipuss resolution through a process known as transference. This involves transferring large sums of money, as you DISCOVER what you are, to the therapist via VISA.

Cheaper you want? I recommend Primal Meow Therapy—even though it cuts into my business.

References

Zimmer, Medea (342 BC). *Collected Letters to Her Children, (including "So Why Couldn't You Even Phone Me Once in a While?")* Scrollier's

Annie, Orphan (1936). *"Oh, Daddy! Oh, Daddy! Leapin' Lizards!"* Elektrolux Books.

Chapter 6

Littermate Rivalry

Littermate rivalry among cats corresponds to sibling rivalry among humans and is characterized by fierce competition between kittens born to the same parents. Jealousy, resentment and anger fuel these dysfunctional relationships.

The first literary discussion of the syndrome occurs in a Yiddish version of Snow White, portraying the heroine as resident therapist for seven cats who live in a halfway house.

As told in the old country, the tale was called, *Shney Vays un der Zibn Katzales.*

Because the story was probingly psychoanalytic, dimwitted dwarves were substituted for cats by modern chroniclers of fairy tales. (Given the socially-sensitive and politically-correct consciousness of our times, future Snow Whites will probably be the fairy godmothers of height-deprived persons.)

Freud was intrigued by the subtleties of the *boubameisa*. In a celebrated monograph, his diagnosis of the seven cats were scathingly succinct.

    Bashful *(Shemevdik)* regressive
    Happy *(Frailech)*: manic
    Sleepy *(Shleferik)*: narcoleptic
    Grumpy *(Farmuket)*: melancholic
    Sneezy *(Nosy)*: hypochondriacal
    Dopey *(Zier Narish)*: autistic
    Doc *(Dok)*: transvestite (because of his
        affinity for frilly surgical masks, long
        white gowns and latex gloves.)

His *Shney Vay* theories challenged, Freud sought to recreate the dynamics of the fairy tale by installing seven birth-related cats and a *shikseh* in an isolated environment of their own, a motel on the outskirts of Deutschneyland.

The cats were named Groucho, Harpo, Chico, Zeppo, Bimbo, Osso and Buco.

Freud, often referred to as the Einstein of psychoanalysis, encouraged the cats to act out their emotional conflicts but refused to intervene therapeutically.

Every night he hypnotized the cats with Don Ameche movies and coaxed the kittens to reveal their innermost feelings toward each other. Their criticisms were merciless. Here is a severely edited transcript of remarks by Osso:

    . . . Chico won't let us watch anything on TV except
    the Playboy Channel.

   . . . Bimbo does not wash all over, especially the tail part.
   . . . Zeppo never uses the clean part of the litter box.
   . . . Harpo howls at the moon while touching himself you know where.
   . . . Groucho steals cigars from the humidor of you know who.
   . . . Buco steps on cracks to break mother's back.
   . . . All of my brothers and sisters have *ka-ka* for brains.

In summing up the results of his controlled study, Freud concluded, "These cats are nuttier than *fruchtkuchen*. Why? Because *Shney Vay* is no substitute for a real mother. Not even a good *balabusta!* She spends all of her time at the harpsichord playing, 'Whistle While You Work,' She is Barbie Doll waiting for a nervous breakdown to happen.

Among his other findings:

1. Littermate rivalry may occur between toms, queens or those who are undecided.
2. Within a family, littermate rivalry may be contagious.
3. The rivalry may last for 10 seconds to 75 years.
4. In Mexico, the condition is most common among Hispanics.
5. Sibling rivalry rarely affects the cat who is an only child.
6. If a sibling inherits more money than his/her brothers and sisters—*oy gevalt*.
7. *Shney Vay* dyed her hair. "By the roots, I can tell."
8. To foil pursuit by a wolf, a peasant will toss his children, one by one, from the back of his sleigh.

The last remark puzzled Freud's peers and Freud himself. "I heard it from Turgenov, the writer, one night when he was *kaput* with the *schnapps*."

Chapter 7

Cats Who Love Too Much

**by Judi Wright Lashnits, Cat Writers' Association
Mt. Kisco, NY**

Does your cat love you too much? Or is your cat normal in that it aloofly tolerates you as the *shlump* who will open cans of cat food and change the litter often enough to avoid condemnation by the Board of Health?

Take the test below and set your mind at ease—or on edge.

1. Does your cat suck *its* thumb or *yours?*
2. Has your pet so conned you with love that the title to your house is the cat's name?
3. Does your pussycat sit in your lap when you

are on the potty— and oversee all aspects of your grooming?
4. Does your cat want to celebrate Valentine's Day 365 times a year?
5. Does your cat dote on "cooking" dinner for you even though you detest dry pellets and "savory" kidney mixed with fish?
6. Does your cat decide when both of you will slumber, snack, play or engage in any other activity?
7. Do you and your cat go on double dates together? (Does your cat *allow* you to date?)
8. Does your cat insist that you wear an electronic surveillance collar?
9. Does you cat sit on the edge of the tub and sing with you while you shower?
10. Does your cat heel when it walks with you from room to room?

If you answered yes to more than one question you are accursed with a cat who loves you much too much. And here's the kicker: you are to blame. According to psychiatrists, you subconsciously crave being the cat's idol and slave. Further, you have encouraged—nay, enabled—the cat to become addicted to you and seize control of your life. Such a relationship is called "codependency" by shrinks.

Hemingway wrote a book on the subject. It was about a cat who became hooked on and at the mercy of a fish he had hooked. The work was titled *"The Old Manx and the Sea."*

"The Pick Me Up or Else" Syndrome

This cat trains its owner to pick it up and carry it around all day. It does this by biting the human's ankles as around all day. It does this by biting the human's ankles as soon as he or she walks into the room, forcing the person to pick it up, at which time it promptly stops biting and scratching, and starts purring like, well, a kitten. When returned to the floor, the cat resumes biting and scratching until it is picked up again. (A strap–on baby carrier for your cat may prove useful but don't answer the doorbell in this condition, especially if your neighbors know you are frustratingly childless.)

The "Three-Stroke Cat" Syndrome

Many cats show their overwhelming love by biting the hand that pets them. This phenomenon has been studied by scientists but no precise cause has as yet been determined. No one knows why the cat is smiling at you adoringly while you stroke it once, then twice, only to be savagely bitten on the "thrice."

What to do? Put on a glove and determine by trial and painful error whether you have a three-stroke, five-stroke, or, G-d forbid, no stroke cat. If the cat isn't totally predictable, you might be better off forgetting the petting routine. Just say "nice kitty" and leave it at that. But you won't because you are an empowering partner in an unhealthy relationship.

"I Want What I Want When I Want It" Syndrome

The overly empowered cat is usually able to acquire significant rights in the household, well beyond the pillow and bed space it will defend. The cat has the run of the house, will sit at (or on) the table at dinner and has trained its owner to cook exotic regional dishes.

The controlling cat may command its owner to prepare

on a regular basis "vole molé," a small rodent roasted and served with a spicy Mexican chocolate sauce. On special occasions, perhaps "rat-a-tat-touille," which calls for a rat to be machine-gunned and served with eggplant, zucchini and sweet peppers. Masochistic owners secretly enjoy waiting on their cats paw and paw. I knew of one who recently trapped birds in Antarctica and stuffed them with nuts in order to gratify her cat's craving for Pecan Puffins, an exotic dessert.

The "If You Go Away, Don't Bother Coming Back" Syndrome

These cats seem to do okay when separated from you, but upon your return from a well-deserved vacation or a business trip, they'll nail you. I know one *shlimazel* whose furry friend welcomed him home by peeing in his open suitcase while he emptied soiled clothing into a laundry hamper.

"An obvious case of Izzy seeing a rectangular box with interesting smells, and mistaking it for an additional litter box," I ventured.

"My clothes don't smell *that* interesting," said my friend. "*Katzale* is punishing me for going away!" Well, who's to say?

The "Nobody Shoves Me Off My Person's Bed" Syndrome

Many cats don't cope well with change, but the codependent cat isn't about to take it lying down. A cat named Seymour discovered a man sleeping in her mistress's bed one morning. Worse, he was taking up space on Seymour's own pillow. The cat retaliated by hopping up on spraying. It was a safe bet that the cat wasn't mistaking the boyfriend for a litter box.

The "I Won't Share You With Anyone" Syndrome

Cats who love too much refuse to share their owners with anyone, especially other animals or children. I know a cat who invariably attacked her owner when she petted another cat. Perverse, indeed, is the love of the codependent feline.

If my horrifying scenarios have persuaded you that you are possessed not by a demon but by a codependent cat, what should you do about it? Here are some suggestions:

1. Arrange a personality transplant for your cat. It's not easy finding a brain donor but *gelt* talks.
2. Divert the cat's attentions to you by introducing a formidable new member into the household; for openers, a silverback gorilla.
3. Join a support group for people controlled by power-crazed cats.
4. Turn your life over to a Higher Power.
5. Pray for a miracle.

Judi Lashnits and Dr. John C. Wright, are co-authors of *"Is Your Cat Crazy?"* (Available in hardcover and paperback from Macmillan.)

Chapter 8

Case History of an Idiot Savant

by Arthur W. Johnson, Jr., Director
Fleischmann Planetarium, University of Nevada

My introduction to Hubbleh began with a phone call from Dr. Kraft Mayo-Ebbing, the veterinarian who keeps tabs on the health status of my two tabbies, Super and Nova, remarkable cats in that they regularly forecast lunar and solar eclipses by playing dead and covering their eyes with their paws.

The doctor got straight to the point. "Art, I have a patient, a domestic short hair. The cat says he can pinpoint the location of any natural or man-made object in space—

"Not in a zillion millennia" I said. "Utterly impossible! And what do you mean by 'the cat says'"?

"The cat talks to his owner telepathically. Honest!"

"Are you making this up?" I asked, glancing at my calendar. It *wasn't* April Fool's Day.

"Art, I've examined thousands of cats. There's something different about this one. I can sense it. One the one hand, he appears to be mildly retarded. On the other, I'm convinced he really does communicate with his mistress. And he prattles on and on about astronomy. Maybe he's an idiot savant, do you suppose?"

I exhaled sharply. Idiot savants are as rare as truffles in a can of Dinty Moore Stew. They are, clinically, dullards with an inexplicable ability to do complex mathematical calculations, perform intricate musical compositions or demonstrate prodigious feats of memory—e.g., in a nanosecond, recall all of the ex-spouses of the Gabor sisters, Elizabeth Taylor and Mickey Rooney.

"An idiot savant? It's a possibility," I conceded. "But, even with the most sophisticated equipment, plotting the course of celestial objects is like trying to thread a sewing machine while it is in motion. How does the cat claim to do it?"

"By closing his eyes and concentrating!"

"Aw, c'mon!" I protested.

"The cat's name is 'Hubbleh.' Doesn't that tell you anything?"

"No," I replied. "I suppose it refers to the Hubble telescope, but so what?"

"I take it that you're not interested in challenging the cat."

I paused. The veterinarian was by no means gullible. And what did I have to lose?

A few days later, Hubbleh entered my office in the

company of Moon Maiden Moskowitz, a tepee-shaped woman wearing a frizzy red wig, make-up applied with a trowel, a Bud Lite T-shirt and baggies.

"Can I?" she asked, producing a pact of True Menthols.

"No."

"Shit!" she exclaimed and sat down on a couch. "Nice place you have here, but it doesn't look Jewish."

"I don't follow you," I said.

"This *is* 'The Fleischmann Atmospherium Planetarium,' *nu*?"

"Well, yes. Some years ago Mr. Max Fleischmann, heir to a yeast fortune, gave $25-million to the university. One of the grants was for the establishment of this facility."

"So if a planetarium is all about stars, why not a Star of David someplace in honor of Max?"

At loss for an answer, I turned my attention to Hubbleh, an altogether appealing animal, perky and owl-eyed with a feather-duster tail. He sniffed the perimeters of my office, brushed against my leg, strode to my most sophisticated telescope and fiddled with its controls. Then he turned to Moon Maiden, head cocked quizzically.

Moskowitz relayed the cat's thoughts. "Hubbleh says your big-eye-that-says-hi-to-the-sky is *el wacko* and should be recalibrated—like right now."

I was dumbfounded. My telescope had been acting up lately despite my efforts to improve its stability with duct tape.

Smiling cockily, Hubbleh jumped up on a bookcase and stared blankly at Miller's *"Astrophysics of Active Galaxies and Quasi - Stellar Objects," "Chilton's Manual for the Morris Minor,"* Jean Dixon's *"You and Your Horoscope,"* several magazines from The Flat Earth Society and bound issues of *Penthouse Forum*. Then he stretched out full-length on a shelf, paws cradling his chin.

"Let's establish some ground rules," said Moon Maiden.

"Of course."

"You ask Hubbleh to locate the present position of three bodies in space."

"Fine," I said, feeling sillier and sillier.

"Are you a betting man?" she asked.

"Not at all."

"Not even a small wager? Say, $100.00? If Hubbleh flunks even one question, I make a contribution to this place that Max built. And if you lose . . . !" Moskowitz patted the small porcupine quill purse in her lap.

I hesitated.

"*Tokhis afn tish*," she said.

"Okay, if you insist . . ." Raising money for the planetarium is dear to my heart.

"Fire away."

"Well, pretty, little kitty," I began.

"Cut the crap!" said Triple M.

I winced. The interview might prove to be a comedy but, most certainly, not one of manners.

I smiled at the cat and asked him to pinpoint the location of planet Neptune on the 16th of "this month."

Silently, Hubbleh transmitted his answer to his interlocutor: "Three-and-a-half degrees due west of Omicron Capricorni, at right ascension nineteen degrees fifty-six-point-seven minutes, declination minus 20 degrees 14 minutes."

Kaboom! Just like that! Dumb luck on the part of a dumb cat? Still, the odds of arriving so quickly at an accurate calculation are, well, astronomical.

Hubbleh appeared to be dozing off. I asked a question certain to jar him awake. "Now then, what was the date and solar distance of Comet Schwassmann-Wachmann at its last perihelion passage?"

Moskowitz clenched her fists and leaned forward. Her confidence, it seemed, was wavering. The suspense was pinprickly.

"September 22, Greenwich date, at approximately seventeen hundred hours. The comet was then zero-point-nine-four astronomical units from the sun, or 87,420,000 miles, if you prefer. And after its most recent perihelion passage, the nucleus was observed to break up into at least four fragments," from Hubbleh to Moskowitz to Johnson.

I gasped. Who among us has actually witnessed proof of genius—Michelangelo delivering the last hammer-and-chisel blow to the Pietà, Joyce appending the final flourish to "*Ulysses*," Col. Sanders brandishing his *original* recipe? Was another challenge necessary? I didn't think so. But ever the scientist, I decided to question Hubbleh about one of the most obscure asteroids in the entire solar system, a body discovered by my good friend Dr. David Dunham of the University of Maryland.

"Hubbleh, can you provide me with the location of Asteroid 3123 Dunham on May 17th at zero hours' Ephemeris Time?"

The cat stirred, opened his eyes, whiskers twitching, brows furrowed. I longed to hug him and beg him to forgive me for being unfair.

Then he nodded to Moon Maiden. In a monotone, she conveyed his answer, "The asteroid will be found just north of the Teapot in Sagittarius, at right ascension 18h 18.45m, declination -21 deg. 11.5m. Its distance from earth will be 1.522 A.U.'s and it will be approximately 2,401 A.U.'s from the sun. Its approximate visual magnitude, if you care, will then be 17.2."

Wow! I shivered and, on the verge of tears, patted Hubbleh's head. He yawned.

As I escorted the couple to the door, Moskowitz held

out her hand, palm up, fingers scrabbling greedily. One hundred dollars later, I phoned Mayo-Ebbing and stammeringly shared with her the most amazing morning of my life.

The veterinarian listened thoughtfully before posing a question, one I wish I had thought of first.

"Can Hubbleh's powers be employed for the betterment of mankind? Isn't there someway to utilize his incredible gift?"

Here, the story ends, almost. In my zeal to see that Hubbleh received deserved acclaim as, perhaps, the most extraordinary creature in history, I disseminated a news release describing Hubbleh as "the cat with telescopic sight." The media descended on my tiny planetarium. So did law authorities. They arrested Triple M., charging her with several counts of cheating at cards. Her accomplice? A winsome cat as adept at locating jacks as Jupiter, queens as quarks and aces as Aries.

Soon after, Hubbleh disappeared from sight, quite literally—in a spacecraft sponsored jointly by the Republic of Malawi, Tang for Tabbies, Surefit Pampers for Pussycats and The Primal Meow Institute. Purriodically, Hubbleh corrects the observations of astronomers on planet earth and elsewhere, but from cyberspace he sends word that he's lonely.

According to my notes, his last address was Gamma Hydrae at R.A. 13h 20.5, dec. minus 25d. 14m., just past Mars' orbit in a highly elliptical orbit. Visiting hours are from 10 A.M. to 5 P.M., daily only—except on Shabbes and high holy days. (In the case of Hubbleh, very, very high.)

Chapter 9

Past Life Recall and Possession

Trauma in a cat's previous lives often account for a cat's dysfunctionality in its present life.

As all cats have nine lives, it is likely that your cat has already lived one or more of them. Curiously, there may be gaps of decades or centuries between each life. The hypnotist Von Fleigenkloppfer recorded the lives of a cat who lived as a morel in the Devonian period, a hippocampus in the Cambrian period and a meter maid when Fiorello LaGuardia was mayor of N.Y.C.

Under hypnosis, many cats can recall previous lives in uncanny detail. Such a cat was Moishe, a Sealpoint Siamese and the most unforgettably famous ex-person I have ever interviewed.

The cat's owners, Reuben and Myra Shiff, claimed Moishe could read Hebrew and speak Yiddish.

"What makes you think so?" I asked when they implored me to investigate their pet's previous lives.

"One day when I was angry about something, I used curse words," said Mr. Shiff. "My wife said swearing is a big no–no." And I said, *'Vu shtet es gesreiben?'* Our cat Moishe knew at once I had asked, 'Where is it written?' He immediately consulted the Talmud and the Torah and showed me the passages referring to blasphemous language."

The Shiffs provided many other anecdotes that suggested the cat had once been a Talmudist or Rabbi—but the biggest surprise was yet to come.

Under hypnosis, Moishe said he was born in N.Y.C., in 1779 as Clement Clarke Moore, the only child of Benjamin Moore and his wife Charity.

"Were you Jewish?" I asked.

The cat seemed troubled by the question.

"Yes and no," he answered. "My father was the second Episcopal Bishop of New York but I became a Hebraist and educator."*

"Never mind your 'yes and no,'" I said. "What did your peers regard you as? A Hebraist or an Episcopalian?"

"Sadly, my contributions as a Hebrew scholar were overlooked because I had written a *goyish shtick* for my children." The svelte Siamese twitched uncomfortably.

"What kind of 'shtick?'" I asked.

"Well, it was a poem called, *'A Visit from St. Nicholas.'"*

---

* True facts you can look up in the library. In 1809, Moore published *A Compendious Lexicon of the Hebrew Language: In Two Volumes*. We kid you not!

"Are you putting me on or what?" I asked. "I don't believe you're sharing a past life with me. A fantasy, maybe."

"Would you be convinced that I am being honest if I recited the poem I wrote in 1822 in English—*and* Yiddish?"

By the end of our hypnotic session I was convinced that the elegant cat on my couch had indeed been Clement Clarke Moore. Who else could have written this *goyisha-yiddisha* masterpiece?

A *Chanukah Story?*

'Twas the night before *Chanukah, boychiks* and *maidels,*
Not a sound could be heard, not even the *dreidls.*

The *menorah* was set by the chimney alight,
In the kitchen, the *bubbie* was choppin' a bite:
Salami, pastrami, a *glassele tay,*
And *zoyereh* pickles with *bagels—oy vay!*

Gasundt and *geshmack* the *kinderlach* felt,
While dreaming of *taglach* and *Chanukah gelt.*

The alarm clock was setting a *klappen* and *ticken,*
And *bubbie* was carving a *shtiki* chicken.
A *tummel* arose like a thousand *shmuesses,*
Santa had fallen and broken his *tuchis.*
I put on my slippers—*ains, zvei, drei*—
While *bubbie* was enjoying her herring and rye.
I grabbed for my bathrobe and buttoned my *gotkies,*
And *bubbie* was just devouring the *latkes.*

To the window I ran and to my surprise,
A little red *yarmulke* greeted my eyes.
When he got to the door and saw the *menorah,*
"*Yiddishe kinder,*" he said "*Kenahorah!*
I thought I was in a strange *hoise.*
As long as I'm here, I'll leave a few toys."

"Come into the kitchen, I'll get you a dish,
A *gupel,* a *leffel,* a *shtikele* fish."
With smacks of delight, he started his *fressen,*
Chopped liver and *knadlach* and *kreplach gegessen.*
Along with his meal he had a few *schnappes.*
When it came to eating, this boy was tops.

He asked for some *knishes* with pepper and salt.
But they were so hot he yelled, "*Oy gevalt!*"
He buttoned his *kapote* and ran from the *tish,*
"Your *koshereh* meals are simply delish."

As he went through the door, he said, "See you later,
I'll be back next *Pesach* in time for the *Seder.*"

More rapid than eagles, his prancers they came,
As he whistled and shouted and called them by name,
"Now, Izzy! Now, Morris! Now, Louis and Sammy!
On Irving and Maxie and Hymie and Manny!"

He gave a *geshrey* as he drove out of sight,
"A good *yontiff* to all and to all a good night!"

Feline Dysfunctionality
Caused by Possession

There is abundant evidence that cats are sometimes possessed by demons or *dybbuks* who enter the animals' bodies and drive the poor cats *meshugeh*. This will not come as a surprise to cat owners who have seen their pets pitch cat fits for no apparent reason. Fortunately possession is a rare phenomenon—although naming a kitten Satan is inviting trouble.

One of the most interesting cases of possession was reported by the Viennese shaman Von Fleigenkloppfer, undeniably the Freud of feline dysfunctional behavior.

Elmo's Fires

Elmo, a common taverna cat, was the boon companion of Pomegranatos, a goatherd and lyrist who lived in the foothills of ancient Sparta with Henrietta Cherkis, a cultural transfer student from the Julliard School.

Henrietta first heard Pomegranatos play his lyre one sun-dappled day after they had picked wild MSG growing on the mountainside, leaving Elmo to look after the goats. (Under hypnosis, Elmo later recalled that the tune Pomegranatos chose to play was a silly ditty titled, "Death to the Turks.") By chance, Henrietta glanced at the valley below and was astonished to see blue fire coursing up and down Elmo's whiskers and feathery tail.

"Your cat! Take a look! Such fire. If it spreads, he'll be wearing a blazer!"

Pomegranatos shrugged. "Fire happens," he said.

Fires continued to happen to Elmo—and whisker–and–tail–transplants do not come cheap even when purchased with drachmas. At length, the goatherd had his cat examined by Von Fleigenkloppfer who was making house calls in the Mediterranean, accompanied by two donkeys, one for himself and one for a couch.

Elmo's treatment lasted for months and, for the most part, consisted of Primal Kvetch Therapy, sitz baths and flameproofing. When the goatherd had run out of money, the therapist reached a diagnosis.

"The problem is that your cat is Jewish and possessed by a *dybbuk*. The demon must be exorcised by a rabbi who has been trained to 'de-possess' the victim." With this, the Austrian reached in his valise and produced a yarmulke and a business card. "You are one lucky goatherd to have Rabbi Von Fleigenkloppfer at your service."

"But why does the *dybbuk* cause Elmo to catch fire?" asked Henrietta. Fleigenkloppfer cupped his hand to the girl's ear, and whispered, "The Jewish demon is angry with this little Jewish cat because he was never circumcised."

Again, Von Fleigenkloppfer reached into his valise, producing a degree from the Utrecht College of Surgery and a pair of pinking shears.

How to Tell if Your Cat is Possessed or Regressed

To determine if your cat is inhabited by another creature, answer yes or no to these questions:

Does your cat—

1. Receive e-mail from Alpha Centauri I?
2. Tree raccoons and bark at them?
3. Rob graveyards during thunderstorms?
4. Salute gas station pumps and speak in an unknown tongue?
5. Drink from watering holes and shed quills?
6. Insist on sleeping in a casket?

7. Have more than one umbilical cord?
8. Collect Egyptian chariots and lick them all over?
9. Burst into flames while passing wind?
10. Turn appliances on and off by blinking at them?

If you answered yes to any questions, contact the cat's previous owner and ask that person to *re*–"possess" your pet.

References

Seiler, Eddie (1940). I Don't Want to Set the World on Fire. Copyright by *Benjamin & Marcus.*

Pomus & Shuman (1961). His Latest Flame. *Rightsong Music, Publisher.*

Porter, Cole (1949). Too Darn Hot. *Chappell & Co., Inc.*

Chapter 10

Multiple Puss-onalities

by David Pierpont Mogen, M.D.
A Specialist in Aberrant Animal Behavior

    I had never considered making a house call until I received an intriguing letter from Hornisse Z., of Staten Island, NY. She wrote, "My cat, 'Tiger' by name, thinks he is several different people. I kid you not.
    "I would bring him to your office but he will not leave the house. Besides, I am sitting *shiva* for a goldfish who died yesterday and I have two others who look green

around the gills. Could you come here and examine Tiger? Would your fee include ferry fare?"

The following week I called on Hornisse at her dowdily cheerful boarding house.

Long a widow, Hornisse was a massive, mustached hausfrau who augmented her income by bronzing baby shoes and cradle caps. I was somewhat taken aback by her frivolous attire: swath upon swath of besequined spandex and field glasses dependent on a silken cord. (Field Marshal Rommel in drag as coutured by Christo!)

Over *kaffee* laced with *holunderbeere* brandy, Hornisse described the alter egos of her delusional cat.

"My cat? Oy . . . ! He thinks he is all the people who work in a department store on New York City's lower east side in 1931—a *schlumperdik* store—not nice like Bloomie's or Barney's."

"How many people are there—or is he?"

"Seven—no, make that six. Yesterday Tiger fired himself from sporting goods. Why? By me it makes no difference."

Tugging at her forelock, Frau Z., furnished me with capsule descriptions of Tiger's interior *dramatis personae*:

> *Yossi Edelmann*, who rose from pushcart peddler to owner of a department store on Manhattan's lower east side.
>
> *Ginger Peché*, complexion-flawed clerk in notions and dry goods who enjoys fornicating in the freight elevator with Pindaro.
>
> *Pindaro*, teenage stockboy who screws Ginger rather than lose his sight or grow hair on his hands as a result of self abuse.

Brunhilde, bookkeeper and buyer who has not had a raise in 17 years but secretly adores Edelmann.

Lionel Trane, mens' apparel, toy department and gofer.

Chiang Kai-Shekel, Chinese-Jewish chef in the Emporium's deli.

Our interview over, Hornisse led me to the basement and down a hallway to a door marked *Verboten!*
"You want Tiger? Go right in. See you later, *alligator!*" she added, using the Yiddish word for alligator.
I knocked. No answer. Gently, I opened the door. Tiger, wearing a headset, sat at an ancient switchboard. Phone lines writhed from the monster like Medusa's locks. Clouds of dust all but obscured the cat and cobwebs glimmered dimly in the corners.
"*Shalom,*" I said.
Like Brigadoon emerging from the mist, the cat, striped and ferret-faced, rose magisterially.

TIGER AS EDELMANN
(a cackling old man)
Aleichem shalom. May I help you?
(He adjusts the switchboard's speaking tube.)

ME
I'd like to talk to you.

TIGER AS EDELMANN
So talk. Maybe about a suit. A 40-medium, I'd say.
(He plugs into a phone jack.)

Lionel, what you got in a 40 medium? I'm thinking sharkskin. Or maybe Cheviot twill.

TIGER AS LIONEL
(a voice dripping with weltschmerz)
We got from nothing, but we could let out a 38 vest and coat by moving the buttons. *Nu?*

TIGER AS EDELMANN
My tailor tells me we just sold the last 22 garments in your size to the Sultan of Brunei, a regular customer. How about something very nice for the missus?
(He plugs into another phone jack)

Ginger? Hello, Ginger. Ginger?
(He switches phone lines.)

Lionel, go find Ginger! The little hooker is probably going up and down in the freight elevator with Pindaro.
(Tries another phone line.)

Pindaro! Are you and Ginger futzing around?

TIGER AS PINDARO
(who sounds like Marlon Brando)
I'm an Italian, you know? But a Casanova? Hey!

ME
Tiger, perhaps —

TIGER AS EDELMANN
You're calling Mr. Edelmann a 'tiger?' Listen, I'm only trying to make a living by making people happy.
(He pretends his phone has just rung.)

TIGER AS GINGER
(in a nervous, twittery voice)
You called, Mr. Edelmann?

TIGER AS EDELMANN
How come you're *fumfering* like you're out of breath?
(He winks at me lewdly.)

Tell me, *bubeleh,* what's on special today?

TIGER AS GINGER
This you won't believe—a heart-shaped crystal flacon with atomizer. It has two chambers. One contains "Desire," a perfume made from frangipani and attar of wild Irish rose. One whiff and your swain falls to his knees and pledges his troth. Now, are you ready for this?

TIGER AS EDELMANN
Try me.

TIGER AS GINGER
In the other chamber, "Expire," a deadly gas—like from beans and borscht! If your date is getting fresh—poof!—and with one *schpritz* it's goodbye, Mr. Fooling–Around–with–the–Hands–Guy. Only $3.00 including gift wrap and a washable body bag.

ME
Please, Mr. Edelmann, I came here because—

TIGER AS EDELMANN
Because you're hungry. Am I right? Boy, did you come to the right place! You don't know from deli until you've tried ours. It's run by Chiang Kai-Shekel, my chef. I got

him in a hostage trading situation—but it cost me a Rabbi.
(He plugs in a phone line.)

Hello, litchi nut? What's cooking?

TIGER AS CHIANG-KAI-SHEKEL
(a tenor who pauses between words)
Today, all new! For appetizer, dum tsimmes, followed by moo goo kugel, sweet-and-sour kraut, dragon moon fishes in knishes. For dessert, misfortune cookies you would die for!
(Tiger transfers to another line)

TIGER AS EDELMANN
Brunhilde, what's been reduced so drastically that I will probably go bankrupt?

TIGER AS BRUNHILDE
(with throaty Tallulah Bankhead baritone)
Oh, I was just hoping y'all would call, Mr. Edelmann. Isn't it a be-yoo-tiful day?

TIGER AS EDELMANN
For shmoozing I have no time. Please, the markdowns?

TIGER AS BRUNHILDE
Alright, already. For $14.00, a Norwegian blue fox stole consisting of four skins. *(She snickers.)* Also a cuckoo clock that plays the *kol nidre* on the hour. Reduced to $3.95. Also on special, a Mother Hubbard gown for expectant brides with matching pantaloons and bassinet—all for $5.00

TIGER AS EDELMANN
(He turns to me, claps his paws and bows.)

You name it and we got it!

ME
Mr. Edelmann, you're terrific.

Upstairs, I found Hornisse grating almonds on a blancmange.
"You've made a diagnosis?" she asked.
"Yes, multiple personality. But the cat is happy!"
"Happy, schnappy? *An einredenish iz erger vie a krenk!* Can you cure him so he could be like normal?
I shook my head. "Mr. Edelmann is too old to get another job. And consider that Ginger—and, perhaps Pindaro, too—depend on him as a father figure. Worse, there's his repressed, unresolved oedipal conflict with Brunhilde. Finally, there's the issue of the chef's diplomatic status under the Treaty of Versailles."
With that, I presented her with a bill for $5.00 and an extra $1.00 for a house call. Plus 10¢ for round trip ferry fare!

Chapter 11

Feline Stress Syndrome

by Gail Cohen, Writer, Artist and Urban Anthropologist

Akin to angst and anxiety, stress is the specific response by the central nervous system to a stimulus, as fear or pain, that disturbs or interferes with normal psychological equilibrium. This said, let me tell you that you don't know from stress unless you have been a cat.

What causes feline stress? Just in time you asked because less than six months ago a symposium convened at the Hague to discuss Feline Stress Syndrome. It attracted over 500 of the world's top cat behaviorists. A position paper issued at the conclusion of the symposium urged immediate intervention to forestall a complete collapse of the feline species as we now know it.

Here are the ten top stressors of today's cat identified by blue-ribbon panel of scientists, along with their recommendations for reversing each stressor:

Stressor Ten: Litter Box Neglect

Given today's two wage-earner family structure, ineffective litter scooping has become a serious source of stress to today's cat. Case studies presented at the symposium detail horror stories of owners using enough sand to fill the Sahara Desert. This rising trend is having a particularly bad effect on kittens just being trained, as they are unable to make it over sand dunes taller than they are.

A documented case reported by 911 tells of paramedics in Oregon having to dig a kitten out of two feet of Easy Scoop when its mother could not locate her offspring despite having outfitted him with a beeper.

Though at the bottom of the list of stressors, the Hague proclamation urges owners to be more aggressive about their cat's litter box, and will reinforce its position via a public relations and advertising blitz that will include skywriting, shopping cart signage and subliminal television spots featuring Charo, Mother Theresa, Dennis Rodman, Mr. Rogers and Buddy Hackett.

Stressor Nine: Sibling Conflict

Sibling conflict was virtually unheard of in the days of the westward migration, but today's pace of living has elevated this infrequent problem to the status of near crisis.

Striving to get the limited attention of the mother cat in a fatherless household, many kittens are resorting to unheard of measures to upstage their littermates. Reported cases of nose piercing, refusal to adhere to curfews and back-meowing are commonplace among cats coming from inordinately large litters. And, oh yes, fratricide and sororicide.

Cat owners are urged by symposium members to consider time outs, withholding of treats and lots of love as antidotes for this personality-altering circumstance. Mother cats are being urged to stop at one litter through a new program being underwritten by Planned Kittenhood that rewards females for dropping in at the local Spay and Neuter Clinic immediately after a first litter.

Stressor Eight: Letting Go

Mothers burdening their kittens with unrealistic expectations about succeeding in life are urged to seek professional help before the full weight of the empty carton syndrome is upon them. Fifty percent of all cats, most of them female, are being scarred for life by overbearing mothers who were cursed with the "*noudge* daughter" cell found on the third aleel of their DNA.

A typical case study describes Sadiecat, an ambitious Siamese with four degrees (including one from Harvard Law), juggling the presidency of her synagogue sisterhood with chairing Israel Bonds, Feline Chapter. Nagging, ragging and crying before Passover by Sadiecat's mother in the hopes she might lure her daughter to her apartment in Miami Beach for "just one seder before I die" shows the disastrous results of this stressor. Sadiecat had a complete breakdown and had to be confined to Catview, the nation's top psychiatric center for the diagnosis and treatment of Feline Stress Syndrome.

Stressor Seven: Chemical Dependency

Long a hidden topic, the reality of catnip addiction is now recognized as one of the most profound problems in contemporary cat society. Beginning with casual use in the formative years, Drug Czar Socks Clinton has measured, traced and documented (but never inhaled) the evolutionary progression of drug usage in the United States feline population with pinpoint accuracy.

According to Socks' study, casual use, beginning at the litter box level, is commonplace with a marked fall-off somewhere around the age of two. As the maturation process continues, approximately 24% of the feline population becomes dependent or is at risk of becoming dependent upon daily catnip use.

Legislation currently in committee in both the U.S. House and Senate call for stricter monitoring, growing and distribution of catnip. Though both houses expect to pass a bill before summer recess, Socks has already told Congress he'll make sure his owner vetoes the bill, labeled, "ACT (Abolish Catnip Today) Act. Rush Limbaugh has vowed to chain himself to the White House fence until Clinton agrees to pass the measure—or pass gas, whichever comes first. The Hague Commission has agreed to monitor the progress of this issue.

Stressor Six: Depression

Pollution, crowding, divorce, blended litters and violence are the five most often cited reasons for depression in cats, writes Dr. Ruth Brothers, pre-eminent expert on feline moods. Her controversial work with depressed cats has resulted in her Mewlitzer Prize Winning treatise *Don't Be a Pill. Take One Instead!*

Brothers has worked and studied cats for approximately 40 years. She has isolated, treated and returned to society over 5,000 cats and kittens, most of which were successfully treated with potent medicines brewed by Ishi, who sells umbrellas in the Rain Forest.

"A majority of my patients respond favorably to a daily tab of Tabbyzac, Pro-zac or Con-zac, though whether or not any of them will ever lead drug-free lives in the future is still in doubt. My belief that depression is biochemical is substantiated by the fact that cats I've treated have gone on to lead remarkably successful lives from the moment they've been exposed to their medications," Brothers insists.

To make her point, Brothers offers anecdotal evidence. "Some have become symphony tympanists, geomorphologists and professional napkin folders."

Stressor Five: Abandonment

Fear of abandonment has become more profound over the past decades as the incidents of feline date rape, assassination and road kill have been exacerbated by urban sprawl and crowding. Kittens once accustomed to being given their independence at an early age are now reluctant to leave home for fear of returning to an abandoned household. This problem is compounded by weary strays throwing up their paws in exhaustion after six litters. "No more!" they cry.

Once this frustration level has boiled over, it's not uncommon for kittens to return home to find that their mother (indeed, both parents if the household is run by a mated pair) has moved to Montana to live with the Free Cats Militia.

To stem the national epidemic of abandonment panic in cats, the commission recommends owners take their cats everywhere. This includes vacations, movies, dinner parties and, in particular, to the synagogue on the High Holy Days. Outfitting your feline with a *yarmulke, Siddur*, dollar bill for the *tzedeka* box and ear plugs to soften the blowing of the *shofar* on a cat's ears can go a long way toward abolishing, forever, fear of abandonment in cats. If you are living in a remote area and cannot locate the items I recommend, abandon your cat.

Stressor Four: Pollution

If your cat has ever come hopping onto your bed trailing dreck, dust balls as big as tumbleweed and carpet fuzz, he or she is living in a polluted environment. Short of calling Merry Maids, cat owners are urged to vacuum carpets more often than once-per-millennium, picking up small objects that seem to attach themselves to cat fur.

Outdoor cats, particularly those living in such urban centers as Los Angeles, New York and Chicago, should wear small safety masks like those worn by Michael Jackson when he travels. Better yet, one piece suits from NASA.

Stressor Three: Competition in the Work Place

A degree from The Wharton School of Finance no longer promises corporate and fiscal success. Therefore cats can mediate the workplace competition they'll face in the years ahead by double- or even triple-majoring. According to contemporary occupational studies conducted by a cooperative (sometimes) consortium of officials from DOT, HUD, Teamsters, ACLU and DOL—not to mention ATF, JUF and UFO—new wave educational preparation programs for felines include the following double majors for cats seeking a bigger bang for their degree buck:

- Law and Fishing

- Rodent Control and Mortuary Science (including *Mikvah* lady)
- Veterinary Science and *Moehlhood*
- Sleep Laboratory Attendant and Participant
- Liposculpture for Fat Cats and Orthodontia
- Dairy Industry Spokescat and Window-Sitting Lookout

To make possible this rigorous training, the Hague consortium has established a fund administered by the World Bank known as the Catforth Prize. Further, Toads Scholarships will be extended to qualifying felines willing to make the ultimate sacrifice and eat British food. At Toads, "toad-in-the-hole" is *de riguer*.

Stressor Two: Fear of Starvation

Readers of this treatise (at least those still awake) are aware that fear of starvation is a true anthropological conundrum in that it touches upon the physical and mental state of the cat in society.

Fear of starvation should also be viewed as a global problem, but, enormous as it is, this situation can be remedied immediately with one simple action: officials have gone to the United Nations to ask that garbage can covers and dumpster lids be outlawed immediately throughout the globe and that swinging kitty doors be installed at every landfill.

Stressor One: Dogs

The ongoing debate between the superior feline and dumb-as-shit dog rages on. No long-term solution for dogs has been found, though great thinkers have devoted hundreds of years belaboring the question that haunts cats every day: exactly why were dogs invented and who's responsible?

Negotiations between Yapper Inyourhat and the PLO (Puppy League Owners) have failed to negotiate a peace, though dog dishes left filled on the West Bank attracted every canine in Canaan, *kenahora*. Consequently, a plan without precedence to remove the perennial prime stressor of cats has been put into place and will be implemented at exactly 08:00 on *Tisha B'av* in the year 5959. A dog call, installed atop Chicago's Sears Tower, will summon canines to six cities where they will be lured on board intergalactic carriers for relocation to Pluto. If this plan is unsuccessful, a separate conference, scheduled for next year, will devote itself exclusively to this topic.

References

Flegelmann, Hermann (1823). The First Obese Cat Discovered in the New World and the Women Who Loved Him. *Fat Cat Press.*

G-d, No First Name Given. The Consequences of Loading Only One Bag of Kitty Litter on Board the Ark (as told by Noah's eldest son). *Shittim Wood Press.*

Chapter 12

Primal Meow and Primal Painting Therapies

Introduction

Primal Meow Therapy and Primal Paw Painting Therapy are effective in treating more forms of feline dysfunctionality than all of the combined therapies discussed in the next chapter.

While other therapeutic processes tend to focus on specific neuroses and often requires exotic agents —esoteric fauna, obscure musical instruments, seagoing mammals—PMT and PPPT are relatively bother-free. More importantly, the two therapies benefit owner and animal alike, bonding both in a special way.

Primal Meow Therapy
by
Urwelt Schreien, Ph.D.
University of Austro-Hungary/Tenafly, NJ

The premise of PMT, often referred to as PKT (Primal Kvetch Therapy), is that a kittenhood full of pain is not automatically relieved by reaching cathood. Early trauma cannot be ignored, forgotten or "worked through" on a purely intellectual basis. The ghastly memories that still lurk in the crevices of the cat's mind must be revisited if healing is to take place.

Psychiatrist/dietician Von Bulow the Obese, acknowledged father of PMT*, said, "Show me a sour puss and I will prove that the cat's infancy was *ferblunjit*." His battle cry was, "PMT—when talk is not enough." Here is one of his most celebrated case histories:

Case History #458

A white, shorthaired cat with a large, black dot between his ears, Spot lived with Dick and Jane Loeb in an upscale drydock in Mystic Seaport, CT.

---

* Von Bulow conceptualized PMT when, quite by chance, he observed a diapered leopard drink milk from a baby's bottle and cry "Mommy!" and "Daddy!" until he threw up on an elephant. In the 1960's, American psychiatrist Arthur Janov modified the technique for human use and packaged it as "Primal Scream Therapy." Among his first patients were two very cool cats, John Lennon and Yoko Ono. Van Bulow branded Janov a "copycat," and refused to attend Beatles concerts.

Dick was an architect and arc welder who converted war surplus aircraft carriers into Hadassah gift shops— —department stores, actually! (In the "hold," layaway; ninth deck, casual wear; eighth deck, better dresses—and so on. The promenade featured bridal shops. Sportswear was displayed on the sun deck and large and plus large sizes were offered on the "fantail.")

Jane Loeb practiced law, specializing in personal injuries and wrongful deaths resulting from exploding jars of Smucker's jams and jellies.

Spot was an in-and-out cat and a *faygala*. He spent his nights out, frequenting waterfront bars, cozying up to stevedores and reciting Oscar Wilde's love letters to Lord Douglas. At home, he befouled Aubussons and Sarouks, smoked Gauloises cigarettes and kept a diary written in lavender ink.

One night his owners, who rarely conversed, discussed "the damned cat," even as he whizzed on an Oriental rug.

> JANE: See Spot.
> DICK: See Spot's spot.
> JANE: Spot must go.
> DICK: The little *pisher* did go.
> JANE: Spot must go bye-bye.
> DICK: Dick has a Gatling gun.
> JANE: Jane has Smucker's Molotov
>   fruit cocktail.

Before they could act on their base impulses, the couple chanced upon an article about PMT in *Kurbis Schmettern* (Pumpkin Smashers), a magazine published for and by German psychoanalysts.

JANE: Spot needs PMT.
DICK: So do we.

Under the guidance of a PMT technician, Dick, Jane and Spot underwent therapy together. The results were astonishing.

Each relived an agonizingly traumatic event that had been stubbornly concealed by superego. Dick recalled being ridiculed as a toddler because he enjoyed checking himself for hernias. Jane remembered being chastised when she peeked at her baby brother's id. As for their cat, Spot relived having sand kicked in his face by a burly lifeguard—and enjoying it.

Reclaiming their lives, the trio parted ways amicably. Dick donated his aircraft carriers and services to Greenpeace, Spot became a Rastafarian hair stylist in a salon near Coney Island and Jane sought the merry campus of Ball State U., Muncie, IN, where she held classes in home canning, kosher, of course.

Von Bulow, documented over 1,000 kittenhood crises locked in the memories of dysfunctional adult cats. They included:

#786. . .Cat who refused to attend kittengarten because one of the hallway monitors really was a lizard.
#243. . . Kitten who was forced to juggle hair balls.
#901. . ."Fresser," who, as a kitten, was ridiculed when he overdosed in a blintz factory.
#917. . . A feline infant with a fear of dressage induced by a cat-hating Lipizzaner.
#555. . . A cat who was raised as a refrigerator magnet.

How to Meow with Your Cat

The Primal Meow differs from the hunger meow, the attention-getting meow and the mating meow in that the therapeutic meow is directed at a tragic childhood event and delivered with the fury of Carrie Nation addressing a tavern owners' convention. To learn this technique, the cat requires a role model. Who else but you?

The idea may strike you as being absurd. Quoting Von Bulow again, "If the owner is above getting down on the floor and meowing with the cat, then the owner should be 'put to sleep.' *Mein gott,* don't get me started . . . . "

Here are the basic steps for co-meowing with your dysfunctional cat:

    1. Both you and your cat should wear loose fitting clothing, garments which can be easily washed or incinerated

    2. Therapy sessions should be conducted in a room that has been soundproofed with sod, calzone or silly putty.

    3. Because cats intuit unusual events, ranging from tsunamis to close encounters with space aliens, your pet will pick up your vibes when you get ready for your first PMT session. It will know, unequivocally, that this day, like Passover, promises to be different from all others. And cats distrust the unknown as much as we do. It is imperative that you dispel your cat's uneasiness by getting down on all fours and playing games with the cat, perhaps kissy-kissy, schmoozies, tickly-tickly, peekaboo and hugsies.

    4. When your cat is relaxed and loves you as never before, raise your head and meow at the ceiling, softly at first, then more insistently, the while switching your rump from side to side. (If you can flatten your ears or cause your hair to stand on end, so much the better.)

5. Between meows, urge the cat to recall the most devastating event of its kittenhood. Show anger now and caterwaul, punctuating your yowls with protests, epithets and accusations:

> *Loz mich tzu ru!*
> *Fardrat farblondjet! Trog zich op!*
> *A nechtiker tog!*
> *Gai kabenyeh matyereh!*
> *Hostu bei mir an avieh!*
> *Folg mich a gang un gat in drerd!*
> *Kain einoreh!*
> *A sof, a sof!*

It is but a matter of time before one of your jibes will strike home. Willingly or unwillingly, your cat will *kvetch* with you, your cue to discreetly withdraw and allow the animal to solo. Yes, your pet will wail and rail, whimper and simper, cower and glower, but your *katzale* will be all the better for it. The first session will produce only modest relief but it is likely that with each succeeding session the cat's progress will improve significantly.

As a variation on classic PMT, musical PMT often benefits cats, especially if their dysfunctionality proceeds from long repressed and typically Jewish feelings of guilt. Here are some meow-along songs with repentance as their theme:

> Who's Sorry Now
> Give me Just a Little More Time
> Poor, Poor Pitiful Me
> Boo Hoo
> Please Release Me, Let Me Go
> I'm Sorry, So Sorry
> Angst for the Memory

A final word of advice: During PMT sessions, have an emergency phone at hand. Reliving "the moment of truth" can be so stressful as to produce catatonia, characterized by muscular rigidity and mental stupor. And as you are as likely to be the victim as your pet, it is essential that you provide your cat with the phone number of your next of kin.

Primal Paw Painting Therapy
by
Rose Guggenheim,
Galleria di Arte Gatto, Venice, Italy

Than Primal Paw Painting, there is no therapy as ideally suited to serve as an adjunct to or substitute for PMT which calls upon the cat to meow soul-searchingly.

Some cats are embarrassed by vocalizing their pent-up pain, grief, anger. Others are severely inhibited by the authoritarian presence of the therapist and would much prefer to be their own mediators. For all such cats, paw painting provides a very dignified and private form of catharsis.

Cats have been painting with their paws since the dawn of their creation, but, until recently, their artistic endeavors have been misclassified as "cat marking behavior," the application of visual signs defining the boundaries of their territories.

Now it is known that some cats are aesthetically motivated to express themselves by painting, drawing, sculpting or carving with such materials as may be at hand. Paleobiologist Theo Grumbacher was the first researcher to document cats as creatures who derive pleasure from creating works of art.

In 1966, while spelunking in Virginia's touristy Luray Caverns on a grant from Mountain Dew, Grumbacher came upon a wall painting signed with a cat's paw print and dated

1197. The work, which he described as "ambiguously vibrant," depicted Herod, King of Judea, supervising the curing of a pastrami.

Scientists dismissed the discovery as an aberrant oddity until a protege of Jackson Pollock provided this riveting account of the artist's formative years:

"Pollock abandoned art and resigned himself to starving to death when he failed in his attempts to paint with realism in the manner of Gustave Courbet. One Wednesday, his cat who had not eaten in days, picked up several pots of paint and hurled them at blank canvas in the artist's studio. Weird configurations appeared on the stretched fabrics. Many appeared musical and magical in their cohesive spontaneity. "*Ungepachkit!*" murmured Pollack reverently.

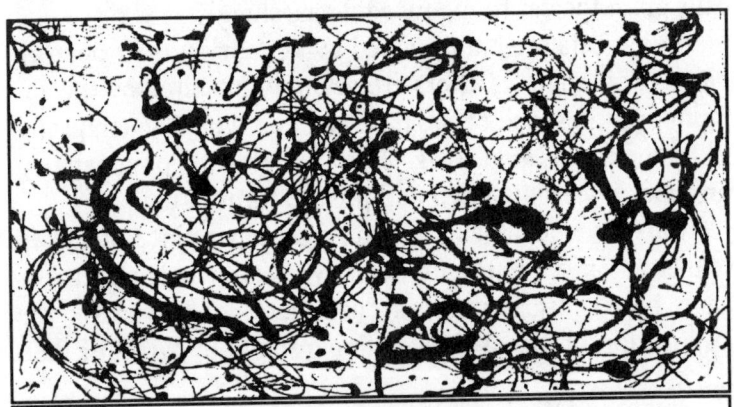

"Potluck" or a Pollock? The provenance of early works sold by the artist divides curators as sharply as a picket fence.

Because Pollock realized that random chance determines whether paint flung from pots creates sophisticated designs or muddy hodgepodges of color and line, he cleverly named his cat "Potluck."

The artist's friends enthused for Potluck's creations and purchased them by bartering subway maps, kasha and tickets to newsreel theaters. Appalled by the commercialization of his work, Potluck refused to "paint" again.

Ever the opportunist, Pollock took matters into his own hands. He purchased a ladder, a slingshot and, guided by a shrewd agent, splattered his name across the emerging school of abstract art by calling his works "action paintings."

Apocryphal though it may be, the anecdote inspired many cat therapists, notably Dr. Dafoe Derailleur, to link feline artwork with Freud's theory that art consists of psychoanalytically revealing dream pictures formed in the primitive mind. Explained Derailleur, "When our waking thoughts are stifled, the savage and the child within us cry out."

In 1960, Derailleur founded the Institute for Primal Paw Painting above a Fotomat in Arles, France. As cats lashed out at long-repressed emotional problems with their paws, whiskers and pointy tails, several extemporaneous styles of art evolved:

"Ash can" school favored by alley cats
Ash-kenazy, a highbrow school of art
Pointillism as developed by Siamese Seal
    point, Blue point, Lilac point and Rose
    Point cats
Haughty pawtraits rendered by narcisstic
    felines enamored of Whistler
Impurressionism and Expurressionism by cats
    with short attention spans
Catacomb and funerary art with which
    Egyptian cats identified
Destructionism, adored by cats with sharp

claws and even sharper tempers
Vos is es? Non-objective art

Apart from boasting an extraordinary rate of recovery in terms of cats regaining their mental health, the school also provided many acknowledged masterpieces of feline art. On view in my galleria on the *Canale della Guidecca*, are such visual delights as:

> I Stalk in the Garden Alone
> Golda Meir's Boogie Woogie
> Shredded Shower Curtain #5
> 'Neath a Farthingale I Wandered
> Bah relief
> Spam Rhomboids in Negative Space

Introducing Your Cat to Primal Paw Painting

Though the urge to paint is instinctual among cats, you may have to prod your cat's primordial memory by serving as a role model.

In an area that has been carpeted and wallpapered with 60-lb tarpaulin, place your hands—curving them like paws—in a tray of paint and apply the paint from your finger nails to a canvas you have placed on an easel, comfortably adjusted to the height of your sitting cat. Apply a second color with the rough idea of a design in mind, then another color and so on.

When your cat's interest heightens, dip your pet's paws in paint and lightly scratch them against the canvas. Your pet will, of course, shake his paws violently as cats do when they have stepped in water or slush but the visual excitement of the splattering effect will not escape the cat's notice. After several introductory sessions, the day will come when your cat will make the connection between cause and effect, load up his/her paws with paint and allow the savage and kitten within to "attack" the canvas.

Cat's first attempts may be of a minimalist nature, but in time your pet will use a multiplicity of effects to explore an astonishing range of emotions.

Teaching your cat to paint with its tail is a task best left to someone astride a mop or broom.

If your cat creates a painting that you judge as being "epiphanic" or "triumphantly ascendant," send a color transparency of the work to me at my gallery. If it isn't just another piece of "cat crap," such an offer I'll make you!

References

Anonymous, Maxine (1997). Me? Ow! Talking to the Kitten Within. *Journal of Primal Meow Therapy.*

Katdinski, Wassily (1941). The Paws That Refresh Us. *Journal of Primal Paw Painting.*

Wolfe, Thomas (1994). Look Homeward, Angelpuss. *Scribner's*

Mewssorgsky, Modest (1870). Pussycat Pictures from an Exhibition. *Purina Pavilion for the Performing Arts, Petrograd.* April 23.

Capote, Wily (1950). Other Voices, Other Wombs. *Amnion Press.*

Chapter 13

Alternative Therapies For Your Crazy Cat

If PMT does not alleviate or correct your cat's behavioral problems, you should consider exposing your pet to one or more of the treatments described below. Some are products of the New Age culture. Others date back to ancient Babylon.

Electrocrystals	Herbalism
Aromatherapy	Acupuncture
Swimming with dolphins	Fire walking
Ear candling	Medicine circle
Holotropic breathwork	drumming
Didgeridoo vibrational	Orgone therapy
message	Zen tap dancing

Therapies to be avoided include:

Lobotomy	Chinese water torture
The rack	Thumb screws
Depilatories	Keelhauling
Sleep deprivation	Mummification
Ducking stool	Crazy Glue™
Knock knock jokes	Taxidermy

Seltzer *shpritzing*

Electrocrystals

Electrocrystals are those that have been placed in a saline solution and charged with amperes. Each crystal has its own healing vibration. After several applications of crystals to its cranial area, your cat may appear electrifyingly normal but its very presence will short-circuit all of the appliances in your home.

Herbalism

Ccats are carnivores. They seldom eat veggies—with the prominent exception of your prized houseplants. So then, consult a herbalist, have your cat's mental health problems diagnosed, buy the prescribed plants and grow them under a blinking neon sign that admonishes, "Not for Eating—*Traif!*" Based on reverse psychology, this stratagem seldom fails.

Aromatherapy for Your Cat

The use of oils extracted from flowers as therapeutic agents has been known to nip many psychosocial disorders in the bud.

The efficacy of aromatherapy was discovered by Vladya Ekk, a flower girl who sold her bloomers in downtown Latvia. She was a simple lass whose costume consisted of buttercup pasties, a strategically placed ranunculus and a yarmulke decorated with Easter lilies. Passersby hurried past the eccentric vendor but stray cats adored her stall, ignoring squirrels, orioles and feral reindeer to stroll about her baskets of colorful blossoms.

Over a period of time, Vladya noted that even the dottiest of cats seemed to become more equable with each visit, and that each of them exhibited a marked preference for a particular species of flower.

One day, while she was sorting out these thoughts, a new cat appeared on the block, preceded by his notoriety.

He was Shtarker, a convicted feline who had spent no less than four of his nine lives in durance vile for offenses ranging from "the utterance of forged instruments" to holding up a codfish cake factory with a joy buzzer, exploding cigar and squirting fountain pen and, subsequently, indecent exposure at a charivari.

Upon encountering Vladya, Shtarker sought to impress her as being a cat with *real* attitude. He spat on her salvia, kicked her cannas and black-eyed her Susans. Tears welled in Vladya's eyes. Then, to her astonishment, Shtarker paused before a display of verbena, sniffed the yellow flowers and underwent a profound transformation. He knelt on all four kneecaps, begged her forgiveness and bade her to join him in a bossanova.

The incident, coupled with earlier observations, led Vladya to the inescapable conclusion that "flowers can perform blooming miracles." Her observation— in Latvian: *Kwz flistwern pyh mglldworgkwpp hoo-ha!*—appears on the awning of the aromatherapy clinic she founded. The facility is called, "Up Your Nose."

Aromatherapeutic Procedure

Essences are applied to the cat by massaging the oils into the animal's skin, preferably along the spinal reflex—and what cat doesn't like a back rub? If you have a hairless Sphynx, the essence may be applied with a paint roller, leaf blower or 400-grit garnet sandpaper.

Aromatic remedies for common forms of feline dysfunctionality include the following:

Negative States	Therapeutic Essences
Cat insists on boiling its litter after each and every use	Rock rose, Gentian box Olive, Cerato
Trashes inedible flashlight batteries stored in refrigerator	Mimulus, Star of Bethlehem, Water Violet
Deposits adult sex toys and dirty laundry at feet of guests	Impatiens, Wild oat, Hornbeam, Cherry, Plum
Feigns starvation by falling down in front of blood-mobiles	Crab apple, Centaury, Agrimony
Won't bathe unless wearing frogman suit	Willow, Vervain, Chicory
Fantasizes about sucking the paté out of live Strasbourg geese	Beech, Clove, Honeysuckle

Breaks wind when passing "Precious Moments" statues	Mustard, Walnut, Holly
Can't sleep without clock showing the time in 60 cities around the world	Larch, Chestnut Bud, Gorse
Programs its love cries into your phone answering machine	Scleranthus, Vine, Heather
Practices origami with toilet paper	Rock Water, Clematis, Wild Rose
Frequently runs away from home	Wandering Jew (*Zebrina pendula*)

Acupuncture

Acupuncture has been a central theme of Chinese medicine since ancient times. Surprisingly, the first cat to be subjected to the procedure was born in this country and century.

An Historic Case History

Pitsel was a scruffy, odd-eyed, white shorthair owned by Mordecai and Zelda Mishkin, a Jewish couple who raised sundry crops including matzos and kosher dill pickles on their farm in Pennsylvania, augmenting their income by posing—pitchfork upended—for Grant Wood and clog dancing on the Lawrence Welk show.

Though devoted to Pitsel, the fervently religious Mishkins believed "kitty cat" had been *geshroft* since birth. Their odd-eyed feline seemed hellbent on rebelling against the strictures of their Orthodox beliefs. She chewed jimsonweed, stared brazenly at cats of the opposite sex and performed the most personal of ablutions in public. Not infrequently she affrighted horses with an "evil eye" and swilled whortleberry wine Mordecai had concealed in a well. One of her proudest accomplishments was positioning bee hives 'neath the rump-worn seat of the communal privy.

Mordecai and Zelda had made repeated efforts to reform Pitsel. They paid a hundred-weight of carved peach pits, some depicting the Exodus, to a TV evangelist who promised to snatch the cat from Satan's grasp. The cat regressed. Came spring, Pitsel suffered convulsions when she was force-fed a cure-all nostrum sold from the back of a wagon by a huckster with a facial tic and a cabbage-sized goiter.

Amulets also proved ineffectual as did the laying on of hands by Rabbi "Buster" Schadenfreude and his minyan who wore matching bib overalls.

Then, one Wednesday, while slopping her faux hogs, Zelda had the first of many recurring visions. She beheld a haloed mandarin holding a sheaf of long needles in each hand, bending over a white, Brillo-textured cat with a blue eye and a yellow eye! Pitsel?

That very week Zelda came across a picture of the wizened Oriental in a newspaper lining the floor of a bird cage. She showed the ad to Mordecai. It spoke glowingly of the skills of Chih-Chih Cha who specialized in curing the ailments of contrary animals.

Hitching up their all-terrain buggy, with Pitsel hunkered down in a burlap grain sack, the Mishkins called on the "Chinaman," a smithy, veterinarian and hotelier who provided accommodations for movers (delivery men) and Shakers (furniture makers).

Mordecai and Zelda recited their litany of Pitsel's sins

and shortcomings. His gold-capped teeth winking in the sunlight, Chih-Chih cackled and reeled, for he was stupendously drunk.

"Well, can you help our cat?" asked Mordecai.

Chih-Chih Cha belched, frowned and murmured "Miao." (In Chinese, the word means mystery.)

Then he bestirred himself. After scrubbing his hands with Ajax, he deftly inserted bamboo needles in the Heaven, Earth, Water, Fire and Central parts of the startled cat, and corrected Pitsel's Yin-Yang balance by playing *"You Always Hurt the One You Love"* on a pan pipe of graduated egg rolls. Within the hour, the white cat was "cured," her distinction as the world's first feline acupuncturee forever secured.

On return to the Mishkins' farm, Pitsel behaved angelically. Years later, the cat recalled, "I had decided it was better to be a good pussycat than a goddam pincushion."

By the following year, however, Pitsel wearied of being a goody two-shoes, or four-shoes, as the case may be. She became a stand-up comedienne and did impersonations of Lenny Bruce and Richard Pryor at Amish nightclubs in Pottsville and King of Prussia, PA.

Epilogue: The Mishkins replaced departed Pitsel with a mute malamute purchased at a silent auction. The acupuncturist Chih-Chih-Cha, betwixt patients, maintained his skills by practicing on sweet-and-sour flanken and turnpike roadkill.

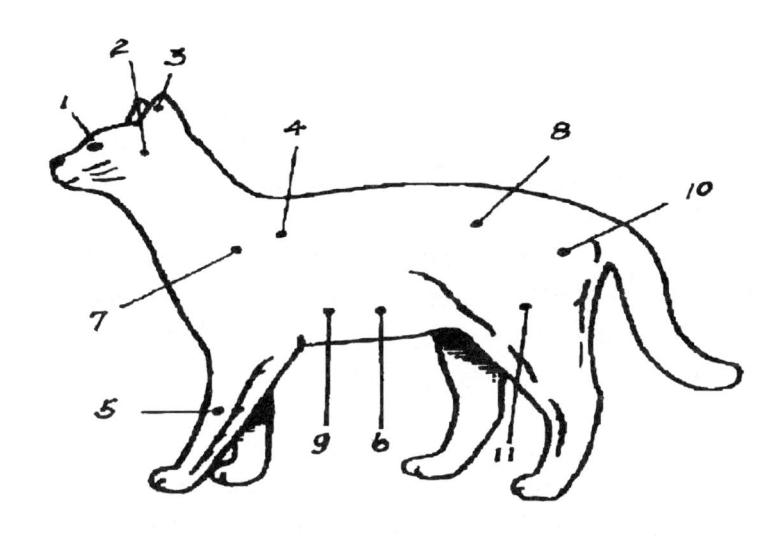

1. Fears xylophonists
2. Chronic insomnia
3. Hears voices: Al Jolson, George Jessel
4. Postpartum depression (times number of kittens)
5. Collects Ninja Warrior weapons
6. Eating disorders—fried pork rind addiction, crudités, art gum erasers, banana skins
7. Kleptomania or faulty pacemaker
8. Delusions—e.g., Princess Di or Redd Foxx
9. Pastrami envy (may include hand-biting)
10. Cannot be weaned from pacifier

Application

Study the diagram on the previous page. It shows you precisely where to insert a sterile acupuncture needle in order to alleviate your cat's specific mental disorder.

Do not practice on your own cat. Use a friend's.

Do not treat your cat at home. Its outraged cries, expressions of indignation rather than pain, will bring irate animal activists to your door—or through your window—and you may not have enough *nosherei* to go around.

"Catupuncture," as it is called, is best practiced somewhere off the beaten track, e.g., self-storage warehouses, Stonehenge at night, Jerusalem's Wailing Wall on non-holy days.

Finally, take note of these professional secrets obtained from three legendary healers.

Pedro Shapiro

So who can sell tattoos to Jews? Not even a *draikop* like Pedro Shapiro, a Jew from Cuba who doesn't look Cubish. Once a tattooist, today he specializes in healing cats with needles. "The only discomfort the cat experiences is psychological," he explains. "It is essential, therefore, to distract the cat from the instruments you will be using.

"Direct the cat's attention to a cockroach fight you have staged. Or a flea circus. Kissing gouramis, especially in a state of foreplay, may attract your cat's attention.

"In the case of highly intellectual cat like the Korat, a challenging book is recommended—perhaps the works of Martin Buber. Three Stooges movies are recommended for lowbrow cats, *schnooks*.

"Once you have diverted the cat, work fast. A pneumatic

needle gun is a big help and can also be used to reupholster chairs."

Mama Doc

A direct descendant of the former slave Toussaint L'Ouverture, this Haitian voodoo priestess advises practicing acupuncture with rag dolls fashioned in the likeness of your enemies. " If you make a small mistake like puncturing the brain, well, good riddance." She believes a cat's behavior problems are caused by *loa*, evil spirits of the dead occupying the cat's body. (See Chapter 9.)

"Before you proceed with catupuncture, try to find the cat. If you are successful, put the animal at ease with Mama Doc's Sonny Liston Punch which I make with equal parts of Prestone Anti-freeze, Glenfiddich, Old English Stain Remover, Sen–Sen and Mogen David 20–20.

"After the cat has been 'stuporfied' [sic], the catupuncture can begin and will prove agreeable to the cat, especially when the needles have forced the *loa* out in the open where you can cast a spell on them."

Employing black magic, Mama Doc turns the *loa* into Maytag washers and dryers which are much sought after in the villages bordering Port-au-Prince.

Jennijoy Tremble née Tsiteren

Sure of hand and eye, this animal behaviorist believes that successful catupuncture must rely on the element of surprise.

"I diagnose the cat, paint strategically placed bull's eyes on the cat's body, conceal myself behind a hedgerow and throw the acupuncture needles at the targets on the animal. It takes lots of practice, I grant you, but it can be done. And because the throwee does not know the identity of the thrower you and your cat can remain the best of friends.

(Here it should be noted that Jennijoy was captain of the darts team at Aberystwyth University, Wales, where she majored in declining Hebraic-Gaelic intransitive verbs.)

Swimming with Dolphins*

Dolphins flip over the idea of swimming with other mammals. The act of paddling with a porpoise imbues the co-swimmer with a spiritual life force called "the wave motion continuum." It is said that the exercise opens neural pathways, releases constricting emotional patterns and relieves dry skin. Dolphins often teach cats how to *hunt ruderen* (dog paddle) before taking them for a ride on the wild side.

Josh Wasserman, Hindustani protégé of Dr. John Lilly, pioneer dolphinologist, popularized this form of therapy for dysfunctional cats by inventing a safety harness and submersible missal for their use.

Most cats cringe at the thought of being towed by grinning porpoises at speeds of up to 30 knots. Wasserman gives cats free choice in the matter. "So what kind of swimming do you want? With the dolphins? Or the 'Great Whites?'"

Fire Walking and Medicine Circle-Drumming

These therapies work well together and are nearly certain to induce primal meows. In Rajesthan, India, the therapies are often combined with elephant polo. The rules are very complicated and penalize cats for spooking the pachyderms or stepping out of bounds.

* Also known as "aqua–energistics."

Ear Candling

Place a burning candle beside one of your cat's ears. Peer in the opposite ear. If you can see light at the end of the tunnel, your cat is empty-headed and beyond help. Some therapists claim candling removes debris from the ear and throat passages, making it easier for cats to yodel Bavarian beer drinking songs.

Holotropic Breathwork

Yoga-oriented deep breathing combined with meditation and the use of a defibrillator elevates the moods of cats who appear "lifeless."

Orgone Box Therapy

Austrian psychoanalyst William Reich invented the "orgone energy accumulator" in the belief that orgone, a nonmaterial element, functions as a therapeutic life energy. He had his patients sit in a sealed box infused with orgone until they opined that all of their mental problems had taken a hike. The treatment was very expensive. Fellow analysts called the moneymaking contraption "jack-in-the-box." Since Reich's death in 1957, an orgone accumulator for dysfunctional cats has been made available by Budd Lake, N.J., Heating & Plumbing Contractors (Occ. Lic. #456691). The firm also sells a basic do-it-yourself kit consisting of a large UPS carton, amusing butterfly valves, lengths of plastic garden hose, a foot treadle and a generous supply of organic orgone. The deluxe model features a commercial hair dryer, piped-in Muzak and old dog-eared magazines.

Of all psychotherapies, this rates as cats' favorite. The prospect of their clambering into a box is irresistible.

Didgeridoo* Vibrational Massage

The mechanics of this therapy from the Aborigines are shrouded in mystery. All that is known is that while the digeridoo'ers play their instruments, the sound waves cause the cats to levitate. When they are collected from trees and rooftops, the animals are unnaturally calm. The same effect has been observed in Swiss brown cows exposed to the pulsations of alpenhorns, even those being played on distant peaks during the filming of cough drop commercials.

Zen Tap Dancing

Cats wear pillows on their feet during this form of group therapy. As the tempo of the music accelerates, pillow fights erupt, relieving the cats of their pent-up aggressions.

* A wind instrument favored by the Australian aborigines and created by nature when termites hollow out the limb of a eucalyptus tree.

References

Noyes, Alfred (1956). Paradiddling, Tom-tomming and Gestalt Bongo for Cats Who March to a Different Drummer. *DVM-AM-FM Review.*

Pearce, Will (1993). Cats on Pins and Needles. *Journal of Radical Acupuncture,* 14.

Chapter 14

Electroshock Therapy

by "Doc" Jethro Lugston, Retired Cat Therapist
Millers Landing, Tennessee

[Note: Self-educated, the author of this essay pioneered a crude but effective therapy in the 1930's that restored sound mental health to many cats thought to be untreatable.]

To tell the truth, the first Jews I ever met were Col. Kornblum and his wife Sheila, and if it weren't for them I would never have become a locally famous healer of cats.

My story begins back when I was working for the Miller Ford Agency as general sales manager, chief mechanic and pumping gas at 15¢ a gallon. Well, late one afternoon this Packard pulled up to the pumps. Great G-d in the mornin', it was a car! Seemed like the front and rear ends were in different counties. And custom-everything—dual "carbs," superchargers, bullet-proof windows thick as the portholes on a bathysphere I'd seen in the *NATIONAL GEOGRAPHIC.*

Turned out the folks in the Packard were the Colonel, a portly man dressed as a mortician—striped coat, wing collar and grey silk tie, spats and a Malacca cane—and his young wife, all rouged up, beaky nose, red dress, stilty legs, yellow shoes. From a distance, you'd take her for a flamingo.

Well, after I had filled the vehicle's oversized tank—32 gallons!—his wife returned from the privy that stood next to a battered Hudson Terraplane we had taken in on trade. Sheila leaned against her husband wearily. "*Ich bin hungerik,* Sid," she said. "*Vu is doh a guter restoran?*"

"Where is a good restaurant?" asked the Colonel, stroking his goatee.

"Well, there's 'The Dixie Cafe' if you're in the mood for catfish stew, chitlins or fried ham with red-eye gravy," I answered.

Sheila's knees sort of buckled. "*Gevalt!*" she said.

"We're Jewish," said the Colonel.

"I'm Baptist myself," I said, trying to be worldly. "And you're welcome to attend our church anytime," I added nonchalantly, although inwardly I couldn't have been more amazed if I had been introduced to a Kickapoo or a Hottentot.

Sheila murmured something, again in a secret language, and the Colonel asked where he and his missus could spend the night.

"There's the widder Phoebe's hotel and bait shop just down the road," I answered.

"*Oy, gevalt,*" said Sheila. Then she turned to me. "I have a very, very sick cat. His name is Jerome."

Sheila opened the Packard's rear door, reached into the back seat area and produced a small cage. Its occupant was a Persian as soft and silvery as dandelion down in moonlight. And Jerome was making more noise than two bobcats in a croaker sack though he weren't much bigger than a grasshopper's fart.

"What's wrong with the cat?" I asked, having been blessed by the Lord with an uncommon gift for small talk.

"Don't get her started," warned the Colonel. "We'll drop by in the morning." A minute later, the Packard took off like a weasel hauling ass out of a pepper patch.

Come noon of the next day and the Colonel and his wife visited me again. While her husband inspected our inventory—three roadsters, a business coupé and a photograph of a convertible on order—Miz Sheila read me a list of Jerome's complaints and I swear it was longer than a roll call of the Confederate dead at Vicksburg. What it all added up to, as far as I could see, was that the cat was plumb crazy. According to his mistress, Jerome would run around in circles until his heart stopped beating, butt his head against the wall 'til he lost consciousness, babble hysterically and sometimes do handstands in the toilet with his head under water.

"Where is the nearest veterinarian?" Miz Sheila asked, brushing a tear from her eye.

"I'll have to ask around," I said. "There's 'Swede' but he mostly shoes mules and horses. And there's 'Painless Simms," a dentist who also doctors pigs and cows. I 'spect your best bet is to get Jerome treated in Nashville. They've got everything up there," I explained.

"Little *katzale* will never make it that far," she said, sobbing softly.

'Bout this time the Colonel emerged. "Say, young man,

nice little town you've got here. But what do you folks do for amusement?"

"There's Rusty's Saloon where a feller can shoot pool, play cards or wrassle in the parking lot and there's the Golden Goose across the street—same kind of layout."

The Colonel twirled his cane and smiled like a man holding four of a kind. "You've been most enlightening."

His wife slipped me five bucks. "Find a doctor for my cat."

They left. I made several calls regarding sickly Jerome but I was about as successful as a one-legged man in an ass-kicking contest.

Jerome's mistress called on me the following morning. I gave her the bad news. "There's nobody in these parts who knows about fixing cats. Of course, there's miracle shouters and snake wavers and Blind Maude the Gypsy who cures hare lips, humps and such. It looks for sure like you'll have to take Jerome up to Nashville."

"He's too sick to travel. I have a woman sitting with him. He's scrunched up in a pillow case with his eyes rolling around in his head."

Changing the subject, I asked her where the Colonel was.

"He's sleeping. Tells me he spent the whole night playing bridge, sipping wine and discussing philosophy with some friends he made in town."

Bridge? Wine? Philosophy? My eyes bugged out like a swamp frog staring into the beam of a six-cell Monkey Ward flashlight.

As the day wore on, I learned that the Colonel was a gambling man and then some. Playing draw poker at Rusty's, he had won $146.00 and nearly twice that at the Goose, shucking down the likes of "One-eyed" Jack Stits, the Garrity brothers, Slim McEvoy and "Blue." Brought his own cards, too. Sealed decks of Bicycles right from the factory and made it a point, ever so often, to lightly touch the grip of a Derringer tucked in his paisley waistband.

The next day brought more bad news. Miz Sheila said her cat had jumped out a window. Luckily, he landed in one of the widder Phoebe's hollyhock beds but the cat's breath was rattling like pebbles in a Prince Albert tobacco can. Next, my boss, Lonnie Boatwright, told me that Colonel Kornblum had spent the previous night hustling pool games—eight ball, nine ball, rotation, snooker, you name it— to the tune of almost $400.00.

"He ran three straight racks on Angelo. Then all hell broke loose. The Eyetalian pulled a knife out of one of his boots. Well, the Colonel whipped out a sword from his cane and they went at it. When it was all over, Angelo was nicked up just everywhere, with his clothes down around his ankles like cabbage sliced for slaw." Lonnie took a long pull on an old ketchup bottle full of home brew and offered me a swig. I accepted.

"Jethro, you've got to persuade the Kornblums to leave Miller's Landing. Folks think we're their friends. That could put me out of business. Worse yet, the Colonel says he has powerful friends in Washington. If something happens to him, we'll have revenooers swarming around here like deer flies in August."

"The problem is Jerome, their cat."

Lonnie spat derisively. "I know all about that. Get that damn cat cured." He walked off. "By sundown," he bellowed over his shoulder.

Well, I sat down in the privy, where I do my most serious thinking, poured myself three fingers of I.W. Harper, closed my eyes and prayed for inspiration. And then it came, tooth by tooth, like a zipper opening.

I recalled that my granpaw Ezra Lee, had gone "mental"

some years ago. He had been hearing voices telling him to do crazy things— like vote Republican—so we committed him to a "palace for peculiars," never expecting him to be released. But a young psychiatrist feller, after trying everything else, gave granpaw a series of shock treatments and pronounced him cured, which he was. (In fact, the following spring he married the teen-age winner of a Miss Rheingold Beer beauty contest.)

Electroshock. . . ! If it cured Ezra Lee, well, ... I called Miz Sheila and asked her to bring the cat over to my place. "What are you going to do to Jerome?" she asked when she handed me the Persian cat wrapped in a black shawl. You could tell the li'l feller was scared. His eyes looked as big as eggs in a small skillet.

"It's a secret," I said. "And you can't watch—no more than you can walk into the operating room at Mercy Hospital."

She left reluctantly and I worked swiftly. First, I set Jerome down on the ground a few feet from my Allis Chalmers tractor. Then I cut two lengths of copper wire. Taping a wire to each of his forepaws, I attached the loose ends to my tractor, one to the axle as a ground wire and the other to a spark plug. There weren't nothing to the rest of the procedure. I made sure the tractor's brake was on, took it out of gear, turned on the ignition and pushed the starter.

The tractor roared to life. So did Jerome. First he hopped this way and that way. Then he leaped straight up in the air and landed cartwheeling. I put a brick on the accelerator so the tractor would idle quicker and watched my handheld voltameter's reading soar. Jerome jumped higher, somersaulting every time he touched ground, his silver hair bristling like porcupine quills. When he started to smoke around the edges, I unhooked him and cooled him down with ice water. After a bit, Jerome stood up, looked around dreamily and purred. By the time Miz Sheila returned, the cat was as frisky as a colt in springtime.

The Kornblums left Miller's Landing the next morning after the Colonel had spent the night cleaning out what little remained in the pockets of the boys at Rusty's Saloon and the Golden Goose. Fact is, he had to settle for an Odd Fellow ring, I.O.U.'s, and a gold chain with a St. Anthony of Padua medal that glows in the dark. But for some reason, he didn't wear it, Jews are funny that way.

Well, word of my success spread faster than skunk scent in a tail wind. People with daft cats called on me from places as far away as Wilmington, Raleigh, Macon and Valdosta. Some days I was so busy I had to zap three cats at a time, hooking them up to Claude Beezley's Ford Tri-Motor Aeroplane.

And, of course, Jerome would drop by every so often to have his "battery recharged." As his mistress Sheila explained, "The treatments drive him crazy but they've kept him from going insane."

And, oh, yes, every year around Christmas I get a card from Pelham Manor, N.Y., that says, "*Shalom,* Doc. *Zol vaksen tsibelis fun pupik.* Jerome." It probably means Merry Christmas or something like that. And right below is the paw print of the li'l cat who made me famous."

References

Kaelin, Kato (1995). Post Electroshock Amnesia: "O.J., Who?" *Blank Page Publishing.*

An "Insider's Guide" to Psychiatric Terms Applicable to Cats

> By order of the publisher, the general public is forbidden to read this chapter. It contains technical material written exclusively for use by animal behaviorists, veterinarians, psychologists, psychiatrists and other mental health care technicians. Further, the chapter contains a sexually explicit illustration. If you are a non-professional and disregard the publisher's injunction, you will suffer a *miesseh meshunah*.

Note to the scientific community: You are probably familiar with most of the definitions which follow. But learning a few more couldn't hurt, especially when you are billing a patient. Treating a cat for an infection might be worth $75.00, but throw in *"limphphoitas"* or *"siderodromophobia"* and—*hoo-ha!*

ABLUTOMANIA: An unnatural preoccupation with bathing or cleansing one's self.

ABOIEMENT: Involuntary production of animalistic sounds, e.g., purring, yowling.

ACAROPHOBIA: A dread of mites, worms and other wee pests.

ACATALEPSIA: Abnormal inability to comprehend. Does your cat always respond when you call it by name?

ACOUSTICOPHOBIA: Fear of sounds ranging from cicadas to nuclear explosions.

AGORAPHOBIA: A dread of open spaces, viz., Death Valley.

AGRIOTHYMIA: The impulse to bite with malice aforethought.

AMUSIA: An all too apparent lack of musical ability, not withstanding the success of David Lloyd Webber's *"Cats."*

AULOPHOBIA: Fear of the flute—and, often, the flugelhorn.

BALLISTOPHOBIA: Fear of missiles, especially incoming.

BATRACHOPHIBIA: A morbid fear of heights, e.g., Eiffel, London or World Trade Towers. Acrophobia means the same thing.

BELONEPHOBIA: A dread of needles and, hence, veterinarians.

CATAGELOPHOBIA: An absolute fear of being ridiculed. Call not your cat a "klutz."

CATAPHORA: Doubtless, your cat qualifies, for this is a form of coma with transitory stages of partial consciousness—which sometimes occur when you rip open a bag of Fritolay potato chips while lying abed.

CHASMOS HYSTERICUS: Yawning followed by yawning followed by yawning.

CLAUSTROPHILIA: An uncontrollable desire to be confined in a small place—especially paper bags, shoe boxes, open drawers.

CLIMACOPHOBIA: A morbid fear of stairs. Uncommon, though not with regard to escalators.

CRENNOPHOBIA: Fear of precipices. Switzerland's Jungfrau. Mt. Rushmore. Dolly Parton's bosom.

CYNANTHROPY: Quite rare. Cat thinks he/she is a dog. Never true of the Manx who knows all dogs have tails!

DAEMONOPHOBIA: A morbid fear of spirits, devils and anything written by Stephen King.

DELIRE DU TOUCHER: A passionate mania for touching things, particularly small objects that can be nudged off tables, desks, etc.

DELUSION, GRAND: Cat believes it is Michael Jackson, Madonna—or both!

DELUSION, MIGNON: A cat who believes his/her parents are monarchs. If you have a scepter lying about the house, get rid of it unless it's rightfully yours.

DEMOPHOBIA: Fear of crowds—and subways at rush hour.

DENDROPHILIA: An irresistible love of trees.

ENOSIOPHOBIA: Cat's fear of having committed an unpardonable sin, e.g., like dragging a roast off the table just before you summon dinner guests to the table.

ERTHROPHOBIA: Cat suffering from a fear of the color red. Also communists.

FASTIDIUM CIBI—or **POTUS:** Feline who loathes food—or drink.

Puss in Boots, a fetishist teetering on the brink of utter depravity. His specific symptomology is called the "Imelda Marcos Syndrome."

FETISHISM: A fetish is an object exclusively used or preferred for achieving sexual excitement. Footwear is a repetitive theme in the annals of feline fetishism though rare among cats who have been spayed or neutered. Other objects which heighten cat's fantasies include mashies and niblicks, undergarments stolen from gnomes. Mont Blanc Meisterstrück fountain pens, photographs of Molly Picon, sphygmomanometers, crayolas, Richard Simmons' dial-a-meal cards and soap bubble pipes made in Germany *(seifblase rohr)*.

GARGALESTHESIA: The state in which a cat imagines he/she is being tickled.

GELATIO: A cataleptic state in which the body is rigid as if frozen, often affected by cats craving attention.

HIBERNATION THERAPY: What every cat would volunteer for.

HIPPANTHROPY: The belief that one is a horse. Few such cases reported among cats.

HYPNOBAT: A sleepwalker.

ICTHYOPHOBIA: Fear of fish, piranhas and fish that are *traif*.

INVERSION SLEEP: Somnolence by day, insomnia at night, an exceedingly rare feline phenomenon.

LINONOMANIA: A pleasurable obsession with string.

LIMOPHOITAS: A psychosis resulting from starvation, common when you try to switch your pet from one cat food to another.

LYGOPHILIA: An attraction to dark or gloomy places, symptomatic of the cat who delights in hiding where it cannot be found.

MANIA, CAESAR: The desire to be absolute master of everybody and everything. Do you know such a cat?

MELANCHOLIA FLATUOSA: Don't ask. Just sniff.

MENDICANCY, PATHOLOGICAL: Obsessed to beg—even for food while *fressing*.

MUSOPHOBIA: To be affrighted by mice.

NECROMIMESIS: Believing one's self dead and acting as if this were true.

OPHIDIOMANIA: A craving for snakes.

ORNITHOPHOBIA: Fear of birds—even Larry Bird.

PHASMOPHOBIA: Terror inspired by ghosts.

POLYPHAGIA: Gluttony. Especially true of Maine Coons.

POLYPSYCHISM: The belief that one has several souls or, in the case of cats, many lives yet to be lived.

PONOPHOBIA: Fear of work, a universal condition among cats.

R-L-S SYNDROME: Difficulty in pronouncing these letters—or addiction to the works of Robert Louis Stevenson.

SIDERODROMOPHOBIA: Fear of railroad trains.

XENOGLOSSIA: Speaking a strange or foreign language -- e.g., cat language!

A Glossary of Yiddish Words and Phrases

A nechtikertog!: Forget it!
A sof, sof!: Let's end it!
ains: number one
Aleichem shalom: To you be peace.
an einredenish iz erger vie a krenk: A delusion is worse than a sickness.
bagels: concrete donuts
bashert: destined to be
bombenneurose: shell shock
boubameisa: far fetched story
bubbie: friendly term for anyone
bubbie: same as above
bubeleh: same as above
Chanukah: Sort of a Jewish Christmas
davening: praying
draikop: con man
dreck: inferior goods or excrement
drei: the number three
dybbucks: demons
Fardrat farblondjet! Trog zich op!: Go drive yourself crazy!
faygala: male homosexual

ferblunjit: lost, bewildered, confused
Folg mich a gang un gar in drerd!: Do me a favor and drop dead.
fressen: eating
fressing: same as above
fumfering: double-talk, stutter, unclear
futzing: fooling around
gai kebenyeh matyereh!: Go to hell!
gasundt: good health
gegessen: go to eat
gelt: money
geshmack: tasty, delicious
geshrey a cry or shout
geshroft: accursed
gevalt: cry of distress or sorrow
glassele tay: glass of tea
gotkies: long underwear
goy: a gentile
goyim: plural of above
goyish shtick: a sucker or naive person
goyisha: pertaining to gentile
goyisha-yiddisha: both Jewish and gentile
gupel: a fork

hamentaschen: small triangular cakes eaten at Purim
hoise: a house (Yiddish pronounciation)
holunderbeere: strong alcoholic drink
hostu bei mir an avieh!: So I made a mistake. So what!
kaffee: coffee
kain einoreh!: May no evil befall you
kaput: broken, ruimed, exhausted
katzale: endearing word for cat
kenahorah: knock on wood
kinderlach: little children
klappen: noise
klutz: clumsy oaf
knadlach: dumplings
knish: dumpling filled with apple, cheese, potato, etc.
knishes: plural of above
Kol nidre: first prayer of Yom Kippur service
koshereh: genuine, real thing
kreplach: dumpling, like ravioli, served in soup
kugel: noodle pudding

kvetch: complain, whine
latkes: potato pancakes
leffel: a teaspoon
loz mich tzu ru! leave me alone!
menorah: traditional nine-branched candlestick
meshugel: crazy
meshugehness: craziness
miesseh meshunah: strange death or tragic ending
mikvah: indoor bath or pool for purification
minyan: minimum of 10 men needed to hold a religious service
moehlhood: those who perform circumcisions
nosheri: snacks
noshes: same as above
noudge: pester, nag
nova: smoked salmon
nu: well or so?
oy: oh or oh, no!
oy gevalt: more or less equivalent to Oh, my G-d!
oy, vay: same as above
pisher: a little squirt
Pesach: Passover
putz: a stronger expression than schmuck
schlimazel: a born loser
schlumperdik: sloppy

schmaltz: chicken fat. Also gooey praise
schmuck: disgusting or offensive person
schnapps: liquor, whiskey
schnook: a jerk
seder: A special dinner at Passover
shabbes: Jewish sabbath
shalom: peace to you
shiva: seven days of mourning after a funeral
shlimazel: a born loser
shlump: sloppy person
shmuesses: chats
Shney Vays un der Zibn Katzales: Snow White and the Seven Cats
shofar: a ram's horn sounded in the synagogue on Yom Kippur and Rosh Hashanah
shpritz: a spray as "a shpritz" of whipped cream or to needle someone
shtick: a show biz routine, a spiel, a pitch
shtikele: small amount of food
shtiki: a somewhat larger amount of food
Siddur: Jewish Prayer Book
smoozing: chatting,
taglach: little cakes dipped in honey
ticken: to tick as a clock
tish: table
Tisha B'av: a holiday
tokhis afn tish: in its less vulgar sense, "Put up or shut up"
traif: food unfit to eat according to Jewish dietary law
tsimmes: a sweet compote of carrots or a big fuss over nothing
tuchis: one's buttocks
tummel: confusion, uproar
tzedeka: offering box
ungepachkit: haphazard, overdone
vaksen tsibelis fun pupik: may an onion grow from your navel
vash-tsimmer: bathroom
vu shtet es gesreiben?: where is it written?
weltschmerz: world weariness
yarmulke: skull cap
yontiff: a holiday
zoyoueh: sour
zvei: the number two

ABOUT THE AUTHORS

The Heavilins live in a constant state of depression, a low-lying desert between Nevada's Virginia and Carson mountain ranges, but they become manic when they play with J.P. (as in Jewish Princess), their Shaded Cameo Persian.

Collectors of antique clocks that chime in unison, Pat, Jay and J.P. join hands and paws everyday at the tintinnabulary stroke of twelve and sing Auld Land Syne, Havah Nagilah and Happy Birthday.

When the "fun Heavilins" are not at home, they are in therapy.

❖ ❖ ❖